Charles & Janet,
Continue to model Jesus in your life and ministry. You will be rewarded for your faithful service.

Reuben

Matt. 25: 14-23

# JESUS:
## The Model Missionary

REUBEN J. SEQUEIRA

InspiringVoices

Copyright © 2015 Reuben Sequeira.

All rights reserved. No part of this book may be used or reproduced by any means, graphic, electronic, or mechanical, including photocopying, recording, taping or by any information storage retrieval system without the written permission of the publisher except in the case of brief quotations embodied in critical articles and reviews.

Textual Note:
Unless otherwise noted, Scripture references are from
the New King James Version (NKJV).

Other translations used:
Amplified Bible (AMP)
English Standard Version (ESV)
King James Version (KJV)
The Message (MSG)
New American Standard Bible (NASB)
New International Version (NIV)
New Living Translation (NLT)

Inspiring Voices books may be ordered through booksellers or by contacting:

Inspiring Voices
1663 Liberty Drive
Bloomington, IN 47403
www.inspiringvoices.com
1 (866) 697-5313

Because of the dynamic nature of the Internet, any web addresses or links contained in this book may have changed since publication and may no longer be valid. The views expressed in this work are solely those of the author and do not necessarily reflect the views of the publisher, and the publisher hereby disclaims any responsibility for them.

Any people depicted in stock imagery provided by Thinkstock are models, and such images are being used for illustrative purposes only.
Certain stock imagery © Thinkstock.

ISBN: 978-1-4624-1115-3 (sc)
ISBN: 978-1-4624-1116-0 (e)

Library of Congress Control Number: 2015904749

Print information available on the last page.

Inspiring Voices rev. date: 04/23/2015

# Contents

Introduction ..................................................................................... vii

## PART ONE

Chapter 1    The Beginning of World Missions ................................................. 2
Chapter 2    What is the Ultimate Goal of World Missions? ........................ 5
Chapter 3    What is the Highest Motivation for World Missions? ............ 9

## PART TWO

Chapter 1    Incarnation ........................................................................ 26
Chapter 2    The Purpose of His Coming ............................................... 36
Chapter 3    Anointed by the Spirit ....................................................... 47
Chapter 4    Prayer ................................................................................. 62
Chapter 5    Called—Sent ..................................................................... 74
Chapter 6    The Great Commission .................................................... 81
Chapter 7    Authority ........................................................................... 93
Chapter 8    Ministry ........................................................................... 102
Chapter 9    Teaching and Preaching in Word and Works ................ 107
Chapter 10   Training of the Twelve .................................................... 118
Chapter 11   Satanic Opposition .......................................................... 121
Chapter 12   Suffering .......................................................................... 133

## PART THREE

Chapter 1    Resurrection and Ascension ........................................... 144
Chapter 2    Second Coming and Missions ....................................... 148

Addendum I      I Believe in Reincarnation ........................................ 153
Addendum II     Are the heathen lost without Christ? ....................... 157
Addendum III    Six Reasons for Suffering .......................................... 166
Addendum IV     Prayer and World Missions: Paul's Prayer Requests ........ 168
Addendum V      One Another ............................................................... 177

# INTRODUCTION

Where and when does missions begin? Who gives the desire and the power to fulfill the Great Commission? Who gives the passion for Christ and the world? Though the word "missionary" is not in the Bible, the missionary movement began with God. A Biblical theology of missions begins and ends with God. Missions is the heartbeat of God. The mandate for missions was carried out from Genesis to Revelation. In the annals of time, God was the first Missionary when He shed the blood of an innocent animal to cover the nakedness of Adam and Eve for their disobedience of His clear command. They were lost and doomed, but God took the initiative and slew and shed the blood of an innocent animal and covered them with its skin. The Bible does not mention that Adam and Eve called upon God to save them. It was His initiative. Their sin and its consequences transmitted eternal death to the human race, for all have sinned and need a Savior (Rom. 3:23).

God is the Father of missions, Jesus is the Pattern of missions, and the Holy Spirit is the Executor of missions! God had only one Son and He sent Him as a missionary! If God was not a missionary God, there would be no Incarnation. If there were no Incarnation, there would be no salvation!

Jehovah is portrayed as a missionary God. David Livingstone said, **"God had one Son, and He was a missionary."** He has always revealed His desire to save. We see the foreshadowing of the New Testament Great Commission given when God called Abram to become Abraham, and that through him and his descendants ***all the families of the earth will be blessed*** (Gen. 12:1-3). The Jewish nation was called to represent Him and His message for the need of redemption to the world (Gen. 39-47). Moses was sent to the people of Israel to redeem them from slavery. Mordecai interceded and intervened for the Jews who were doomed to genocide (Ezra 1-10). Nehemiah interceded for the people of Israel and God spared them. God spared Nineveh with the preaching of Jonah. Jesus of the New Testament is the Jehovah of the Old Testament (Heb. 3:1).

Christ, the God-Man, was God's Messenger as well as the living Message to the world. He is the Essence and Core Theology of world missions, the Example to all who would follow Him in global missions today. Biblical theology of missions is not to be man-centered, based on human needs, whether spiritual or physical. But, it is to be God-centered. Missions is not the ultimate. God Himself is. He seeks His own glory (Psa. 96:4)! We have the joy and honor to participate in the very passion He has for His own glory (John 15:11; 17:13). Jesus seeks the glory of His Father (John 7:18; 8:50)!

Jesus began His mission to the Jews first, but His mission was to the world. In the Gospel, two truths are emphasized: God loved the ***world*** (John 3:16) ... all races, all classes, Jews and Gentiles, in all walks of life, and at all levels of society. Christ died for all (II Cor. 5:15). He was the Light of the ***world*** (John 8:12) and the Lamb which takes away the sin of the ***world*** (John 1:29), the Savior of the ***world*** (John 4:42). In the Gospel of John, *"**kosmos**"* (Greek for world) is used 77 times. He was the ***Bread of Life*** to the world. In the Parable of the Weeds, the field is the ***world*** (Matt. 13:38) and the temple was to be a ***house of prayer for all nations***, not to the Jews only (Mark 11:17). Jesus obtained by His death and Resurrection eternal redemption (Heb. 9:12), for the sins of the ***whole world*** (I John 2:2), as ***the Savior of the world*** (I John 4:14), and His mandate was to preach the Gospel to ***all nations*** (Matt. 28:19, 20). The last great sermon is a missions call ... a call to salvation.

> *And the Spirit and the bride say, "Come!" And let him who hears say, "Come!" And let him who thirsts come. Whoever desires, let him take the water of life freely. (Rev 22:17)*

Secondly, the mission of the Church is simply an extension of the Incarnation of Christ (John 20:21). It is to be endued with the same power (14:12-17). The mission of the Church could only be carried out in the power of the Holy Spirit (Acts 1:8). The Holy Spirit is also the Agent that calls to missions.

So, missions from Adam to the present has been an expression of the Trinity: the Father, the Son, and the Holy Spirit. When God created the earth, the Spirit brooded upon the face of the waters. God slew an animal, thus signifying how man would need a sacrifice for forgiveness. Then God gave the prophecy about the coming of the Seed of Christ which would destroy Satan's seed (Gen. 3:15). Thus, we have all of the Trinity involved in Creation and Salvation.

As we shall see, Christ is our ultimate motivation. He is the ***Model Missionary,*** in His life, His message, and His methods. We shall explore some of His characteristics in defining a Biblical Christocentric theology of missions. Hopefully, we shall make personal applications based on His life and ministry. We shall begin our study with the goal of world missions. God's plan of redemption will succeed: mission accomplished (Rev. 11:15-19; Matt. 24:14)!

# PART ONE

# Chapter One

# The Beginning of World Missions

**Question**: When and where did missions begin?

We talked about the goal of world missions. Now, we ask ourselves the question *"where"* and *"when"* did missions begin? What started all the mission organizations, missionaries, pastors, churches, ministries, outreaches, evangelization, in varied formats from the exclusive outreaches to the sophisticated, the highest class of society, as well to those on the streets, homeless, destitute, some who sell their bodies to survive, and to all in-between? It did not begin in time. No man, no church, or any institution began missions. All originates and culminates in the triune God, the glory of God being the highest goal of missions.

## IN ETERNITY

God had devised a plan to redeem the world before creation. World missions began in a prayer meeting in the heart of God before time. God gave a remarkable challenge to His Son to pray (Psa. 2:8). In Isaiah 53:12, the Scriptures record Christ's ministry of intercession as He **made intercession for the transgressors**. Here in this prayer, the whole earth is included. Some have received its answer, while too many have not! Intercession precedes all mission endeavors, even today! From all eternity, God called us, Christ was the means, and the Holy Spirit was the medium for us to hear and respond to the call of God.

> *Ask of Me (the Father challenges the Son), and I will give You the nations (from every people group, language, tongue) for Your inheritance, and the ends of the earth for Your possession.* (Psa. 2:8)

> *... just as you have granted Him power and authority over all flesh, so that He may give eternal life to as many as You have given Him. Father, I want these whom you have given me to be with me where I*

> *am. Then they can see all the glory you gave me because you loved me even before the world began! (John 17:23,24, NLT)*
>
> *...chosen in Him before the foundation of the world. (Eph. 1:4)*

God is a missionary God! He demonstrated that truth from Genesis with the redeeming of Adam and Eve, to Malachi. He sent Noah to construct an ark **to the saving of his house** (Heb. 11:7). God's promise to Abraham that **all peoples on earth will be blessed through you** demonstrates His heart for the world. When He was about to destroy Sodom and Gomorrah, He sent his angels to find 10 righteous people to spare the cities, and found none, but spared Lot and his family. He sent Jonah to preach to the Ninevites for their redemption. He came not only to redeem Israel, but for Gentiles as well (I Tim. 2:4). God takes no pleasure in the death of the wicked (Ezek. 33:11). In His wrath He always remembers mercy (Hab. 3:2).

Jesus, the only begotten Son of God, is the Jehovah of the Old Testament. He is the extreme expression of God's love to the world (John 3:16; Rom. 8:32). He was given the nations for His inheritance of the earth as His possession (Psa. 2:8). All creatures are under His sovereign authority, given by the Father and purchased at the Cross. No person in whom we speak is not under the Lordship of Christ. Even heathen who pray to receive Christ have had the desire to pray placed there by God. Whoever we witness to, when they respond, is an answer to the prayer of Jesus. Now, we are commanded also to pray for the harvest! We are to join the prayer of Jesus for the harvest of souls.

## **IN TIME**

In time, Jesus continually brought the message of salvation to the lost. There were Nicodemus, Zacchaeus, the woman who washed His feet with her tears, the man let down by the roof and paralyzed, and many others. His vision was not only for time, but for eternity. Jesus interceded for Peter that His faith would not fail. On the cross, He cried out, **Father, forgive them for they know not what they do** (Luke 23:34). The whole world was included in that prayer. For the criminal on the Cross, Jesus says to him, **... this day you shall be with me in paradise** (Luke 23:43). All those being saved, some say nearly 80,000 daily have been chosen by Jesus before time! (Luke 22:31,32 – Peter; John 17:9,11,15,18,20)

> *I sacrifice my life for the sheep. ... The Father loves me because I sacrifice my life so I may take it back again. No one can take*

> *my life from me. I sacrifice it voluntarily. For I have the authority to lay it down when I want to and also to take it up again. (John 10:15,17,18, NLT)*

> *While Jesus was here on earth, he offered prayers and pleadings, with a loud cry and tears, to the one who could rescue him from death. And God heard his prayers because of his deep reverence for God. Even though Jesus was God's Son, he learned obedience from the things he suffered. (Heb. 5:7,8, NLT)*

## **IN ETERNITY**

What is the present ministry of Jesus? The ministry of prayer for Christ is not over. Jesus is still quite busy. The Bible says that He ***ever lives to make intercession for us...*** (Rom. 8:34). He is pleading our cause before the Father. We need it! He has prayed for those to whom we witness. As missions began in a prayer meeting, He is still praying for our mission to the world. He is interceding where His laborers are laboring. We are not alone. He goes before us in prayer and in power. When we pray and intercede, we join Him in interceding for the nations (I Tim. 2:5; I John 2:1,2; John 10:16; 17:9-26).

> *Therefore He is also able to save to the uttermost those who come to God through Him, since He always lives to make intercession for them. (Heb. 7:25, NLT)*

> *Who is there to condemn [us]? Will Christ Jesus (the Messiah), Who died, or rather Who was raised from the dead, Who is at the right hand of God actually pleading as He intercedes for us? (Rom. 8:34, AMP)*

## **CONCLUSION**

Intercession precedes all mission endeavors! Missions is to continue in prayer for individuals, for the church, a city, a nation, and the world. Call upon the Lord for your neighbor, your city, for unreached people groups. Ask Him to open their hearts to the Gospel.

# Chapter Two

# What is the Ultimate Goal of World Missions?

## INTRODUCTION

There are some goals that are presented in the church that are temporary goals, but nevertheless worthy goals; i.e., forgiveness of sins, better lifestyle, heaven, fellowship, good teaching and preaching, answers to prayer, fulfilled promises, etc. The question we need to ask ourselves when we talk about a theology of missions that is Christ-centered is, ***"What is the highest goal of world missions?"*** What is the driving force that should send us around the world to share the Gospel of Jesus Christ? Is it man-centered with his needs of satisfaction? Is the highest motivation obedience to the Great Commission? Is it love for sinners or to keep people out of hell? Is it to have better marriages, better families, or strong churches? Better cities? Better relationships? More peace? Better communities? Or is there something beyond being man-centered? There are so many worthy goals that are presented in the church. But, what is the ultimate? What is the end of all missions endeavors? Missions is the means to accomplish those ends.

## WORSHIP[1]

God is seeking worshipers (John 4:23,24; Philippians 2:9-11; Rev. 11:15; 19:6). The supremacy of missions is Christ. It is Christ who was crucified, resurrected and ascended on high Who is to be worshiped. Missions is to be Christ-centered, not only in its proclamation, but in its ultimate goal. One day every people group will worship around the throne. It is estimated that there are still 12,000 yet to be reached with the testimony of Christ to be

---

[1] Psa. 96; Matt. 24:14; Mark 13:10; Phil. 2:9-11

called out for His Name from all nations, from all tribes, people groups, and every tongue. Missions begins and ends in worship. When passion for God is weak, zeal for missions will be weak. Missions is the means to bring more worshipers to God ... more people giving thanks ... more praise and worship ... more light in our world ... more salt ... and more glory to God!

These are many worthy goals and are but a by-product of the highest motivation for world missions. Rather than being man-centered in our following Christ in world missions, the highest motivation for world missions is having *zeal*—*to have a passionate desire to do all for the glory of God in the face of Jesus Christ and for the sake of His Name.* Psalm 67:3,4 says, **Let the people praise you ... let the nations be glad.** Jesus was moved with compassion, but **His higher motivation was to glorify His Father** (John 17:4). It was to see His Name honored ... for people to see the Father's love and compassion ... His forgiveness ... His righteousness and holiness ... His love demonstrated to the world. That will keep us motivated, even if we do not see videos of horrendous poverty, starving children, or the lost condition of mankind. It is to ultimately to bring glory to God alone! A passion for God gives the desire to make His message of salvation through Christ known in our world in word and deed (Psa. 104:34; 9:2). Someone has said, **Professed praise of God without the pleasure of God is hypocrisy.**

Missions exists because there is a need for more true worshipers. Missionaries preach the Gospel so that men and women will be worshipers of God! When we please Him, we are most satisfied. So when God commands praise and worship, He gets the glory, and we get ultimate satisfaction! When we please Him, we are most satisfied. I am the happiest when I make Him happy, when I am intimate with Him, hear and obey His voice. Again, be a pleasure seeker. Let the Lord be our highest love, your highest joy, and our highest worship (Rom. 11:36).

Worship is the ultimate goal and end of all missions because God is ultimate ... **that all nations ... and all peoples would extol (applaud – MSG) Him** (Psa. 117:1)! It is not man-centered, heaven, salvation, or the works of God, but God Himself. It is to satisfy Himself. God's goal is to be our goal! Christ is our Model. This is the Biblical goal of missionaries, churches, ministries, and individuals. When we share Christ with another, it is not ultimately to win them to attend Church, to be a part of our group, or a Bible study, but ultimately that God would be glorified and that they would be worshipers of Christ *in spirit and in truth*. When Jesus talked with the Samaritan woman who had five husbands and was living with her 6$^{th}$ man, Jesus offered her living water with all of her sin of the past and present. She would not have to go to a well any more at noon to escape the scorn of other women.

The story of the Samaritan woman at the well describes this truth. Why was Jesus there? To win a convert that she might experience eternal life? To see her delivered from her sins and saved from hell? To take away the stigma of her life? Yes, to all of the above. But, Jesus was looking for more. The Samaritan woman at that time was more important than the multitudes. He said He was looking for a worshiper, for ... *true worshipers shall worship the Father in spirit and in truth ... for the Father seeks such to worship Him. God is Spirit, and they that worship Him must worship Him in spirit and in truth* (John 4:23). God desires no more the legalism or ritual of man-made religious systems, whether in the name of Christianity. When someone worships Christ, Satan is no longer getting the honor, but Christ Himself. We turn our attention from ourselves to Him.

## TWO QUESTIONS: WHY IS GOD DESIROUS OF WORSHIP?

**First, is it only to ingratiate Himself or is it for others?** When I seek all for His glory, He gets the glory and I get satisfaction. We know that He alone is worthy of our worship. Love seeks the highest good of others. He seeks our highest good. Worship is expected by God who has given us of His salvation in grace through His Son. He is delighted by the sincere love that comes to Him in true worship. God calls us to worship, not only for His enjoyment, but for ours (Psa. 16:11 – *In Your Presence is fullness of JOY...*)! Worship is the way people glorify God, which is a fulfillment and a result of God's love for us. He loves us so much, that by our worshiping He wants to exalt us to something higher and deeper with intimacy with Himself, the Almighty! The Scripture says that He desires our worship *so that He may bestow blessings upon us (Isa. 30:18)*. In our worship, I am ultimately blessed! I am the happiest, the most satisfied, the most at peace, the most joyous, etc., when I make Him happy in my true worship of Him! Why not make Him happy ... seek His pleasure ... seek His highest good? Worship Him with all of our hearts! He gets the glory and we get the benefit ... that of joy, strength, beauty, peace, His presence, etc. To be filled with the Holy Spirit is to *glorify Him* (John 16:14; Psa. 67:3,4,7; 100:2,4).

> *Therefore the LORD will wait, THAT HE MAY BE GRACIOUS UNTO YOU; And therefore He will be exalted, THAT HE MAY HAVE MERCY ON YOU. For the*

> LORD *is a God of justice; Blessed are all those who wait for Him.* (Isa 30:18)

> *Honor and majesty are before him: STRENGTH and GLADNESS are in His place.* (I Chron. 16:27)

**Second, is God an egotist, seeking His own pleasure, using others for selfish gain? (cf. I Cor. 13:5—***love does not seek its own***)** We ask the question: Who is most worthy, most loving, most kind, most holy, most truthful, most merciful, most forgiving, most full of grace, etc.? When He commands praise, when I seek His glory, He gets all the glory. ***In Thy presence is fullness of joy*** (Psa. 16:11). For the good of others God commands us to love Him supremely, not selfishly, but He benefits so that we may receive His benefits. We praise what we value and what we enjoy. We are blessed when we make Him our highest pleasure! Be a pleasure-seeker! When we call people to Christ, He is satisfied and the redeemed are satisfied (Rom. 11:33-36).

> *Delight yourself in the Lord and He shall give you the desires of your heart. … The steps of a good man are ordered (ordained) of the Lord WHEN he delights in Him!* (Psa. 37:4,23)

> *Honor and majesty are before him: STRENGTH and BEAUTY are in his sanctuary.* (Psa. 96:6)

---

"Worship is the ultimate, not missions, because God is ultimate, not man."
—John Piper

---

# Chapter Three

# What is the Highest Motivation for World Missions?

## TO GLORIFY HIS FATHER—FOR HIS GLORY[2]

What was the ultimate purpose and highest motivation of Jesus, the Model Missionary? What motivated Him more than anything else? Was it the lost, the sick, or the needs of mankind? Was it His compassion? Christ's ultimate purpose in His life was not man-centered. First and foremost, Jesus came to glorify His Father ... to honor Him above all else. That was His highest motivation! Everything that He was, all that He did, and all that He said was to glorify His Father in total obedience to His will (John 12:28; Matt. 17:5). Jesus said that He first ministered to His Father before ministering to others.

The ultimate motivation for world missions is not to keep people out of hell, restore lives destroyed by sin and the devil, to heal marriages or reform communities, to be happy here on earth, to go to heaven when we die, or a host of other realities one could mention. Those are all worthy goals. They are all temporary goals and by-products of missions. The ultimate goal is not in time but it is in eternity!

> *You are worthy, O Lord, to receive glory and honor and power; For You created all things, and by Your will they exist and were created. (Rev. 4:11)*
>
> *Everyone who is called by My name, whom I have created for My glory; I have formed him, yes, I have made him. (Isa 43:7)*

Jesus spoke His Father's <u>words</u>. *I have given them the <u>words</u> which You have given to me ...* (John 12:47-50; 14:10; 17:8,14). *I speak not of myself, but*

---

[2] John 1:14,18; 14:9; 17:4,6,26; 8:29; 14:7-10; Phil. 2:5-11

*the Father Who dwells in me* (John 5:30). He did His Father's works (John 14:10). ... *but the Father who dwells in Me does the works—I do nothing of Myself ... for I do only what I see my Father do ...* (John 5:17; 10:25,32). Jesus came to manifest His Father's glory ... *and I seek not My own glory... but the glory which you have given Me* (John 8:50; 17:22). He was One with His Father — *I pray for them that they may be one, just as You and I are One...* (John 17:21; 10:30). He had His Father's love (John 17:26). *He has declared Him* (John 1:18) ... *to know Me is to know My Father* (John 8:19; 14:7-10). *My doctrine is not Mine but of Him that sent Me* (7:16). When Jesus talked with that loose woman of Samaria, Jesus said to His disciples when they questioned Him talking to her, *My food is to do the will of Him who sent Me, and to finish His work* (John 4:34).

Everything He said or did was in response to His Father. *I have manifested Your Name to those You have given Me ... I came not of Myself, but He that sent Me* (John 6:38; 8:30; 13:20). He was on His Father's mission, not His own! His ministry and message were of His Father. He came teaching and preaching the Kingdom of God, healing, casting out devils, and raising the dead (Matt. 9:35)! *I receive not honor from men* **(John 5:23)**. *I came down from heaven, not to do My own will but the will of Him Who sent Me* (John 5:30). He came to *make his name glorious ... My doctrine is not Mine* (John 17:16). *I am not come of Myself* (John 7:28). *Neither came of Myself, but He that sent Me* (John 8:42). *The words that I speak unto you, I speak not of Myself [of My own authority]* (John 14:10). Christ was nothing that God might be all! He *emptied self* of glory and humbled Himself to serve (Phil. 2:5-11). *And the Word became flesh and dwelt among us* (John 1:1,14; Heb. 4:15; 7:26) *...no man has seen God at any time ... the Word has declared Him* (John 1:18; II Cor. 8:9; John 10:17,18). *I lay down my life voluntarily ... that which is from the beginning ... what you have heard, seen, touched, look upon, and handled ... the Word of Life* (I John 1:1-3; Rom. 8:3; Eph. 2:15; Col. 1:22 NLT). He came to please His Father (John 8:31; 7:28). That was His motivation for His coming and dying. The Father honored Him with His resurrection and His ascension (John 17:24). He was a missionary from God the Father.

> *I can do nothing of Myself, but as My Father taught Me, I speak these things. (John 8:28)*

> *... I seek not mine own will, but the will of the Father Who sent Me. ... I have come in My Father's name. (John 5:30, 43)*

Missions is the overflow of our delight in God—our love of Him resulting in our love for the lost and for world evangelization. That was Jesus' passion … to please and glorify His Father! The glory of God is the highest goal of missions because it is the ultimate goal of God! He *created us for His glory* (Isa. 43:7); the life, death, and resurrection of Christ was solely for the glory of His Father (John 17:4; John 12;27,28; Rom. 3:25,26; 6:4; Phil. 2:11); He chose us before the foundation of the world *for His glory* (Eph. 1:4-6), forgives us *for his glory* (I Pet. 4:11; Isa. 43:25); calls us to do all things *for His glory* (I Cor. 10:31); His aim is that the earth will be covered with the knowledge of *the glory of God* (Hab. 2:14), and in the age to come **the glory of the Lord** will be there as light in the endless days (Rev. 21:23). *The glory of God is the highest passion of His own heart and should be ours as well.*

Missions flows from the fullness of God's passion for God Himself. It aims at the participation in the very passion He has for His own glory! We enter into His joy (John 15:11; Gen. 1:26,27; 3:8; I Cor. 11:7)! Man was … to be like God (Isa. 43:7,21) whose goal is to share God's glory *…the glory you have given to me, I have given to them, that they may be one even as we are one* (John 17:23). With the Fall of mankind (Rom. 3:23), redemption was God's means to make man morally like God again … to be created again in the image of God through Christ! We are to do *all for the glory of God* (I Cor. 1:31). We have *been chosen before the foundation of the world for His glory* (Eph. 1:4-6). It is to be the goal of the Church (Isa. 46:6,7; 48:9-11; John 15:11; 17:24; Rev. 4:11). God's aim is *that the earth will be filled with knowledge of His glory as the waters cover the sea* (Hab. 2:14) and that the *glory of God* will be the bright light of endless days (Rev. 21:23).

To glorify and give God glory is to magnify Him by seeing Him bigger … recognizing His sovereignty over the entire universe. He does not ask any opinion as to what is right or wrong. He alone is just! What is truth? He is Truth! What and who is most loving? God is, for God is love. Who seeks our highest good that we might bring Him glory? God Himself! God reveals His glory in Who He is and what He has done that people from all nations that might give Him glory in loving worship (Psa. 96:2,3).

God says that we have been created for His glory alone (Rev. 4:11). Our highest motivation and goal for missions then is for God's glory, not man. *And we beheld His glory in the face of Jesus Christ* (John 1:14). Our love for the lost must not be detached from our primary passion for the glory of God (II Cor. 4:6)!

Missions is the heart of God. He is a God of missions. He wills missions. He commands missions. Again, God was the first Missionary to glorify

Himself. Adam and Eve were created in the Image of God to reflect God Himself. They represented the whole human race. Because of their sin, the Image was marred. To atone for their sin, God slew an animal as a sacrifice and covered them with its skin: one animal's blood, sufficient for a pair. Missions began with God and will end with God!

God continued to demonstrate His character of Light (I John 1:5) and Love (I John 4:8,16), and sent His only begotten Son to the world! He was compelled by His character to redeem lost humanity that He Himself might be glorified.

When our motive is to please Him and to glorify Him, we will always be motivated for missions, whether or not we see starving children, graphic videos, or poverty in the slums of the world. If we have as the highest motivation for missions the misery of man, what motivation do we need to reach the rich and the famous, in the major capitals of the world, the executives, or the world leaders? What of those who drive the BMW's, Jaguars, Mercedes Benzes? Those who live in mansions? When our motivation is the same, for God's glory, the methods change, but the desire to please and serve God remains the same, whether to the rich or the poor, the slums or those with houses and lands, or to those of every culture, race, and language group. All people need the Gospel ... all need a Savior. Doing all for the glory of God motivates world missions, as Christ came to glorify and magnify God, His Father. Christ will ultimately reign supreme.

## HOW DO WE GLORIFY CHRIST?

We are here to fully express Christ on earth, to glorify Him ... to make Christ present in our world. We glorify Him in seven ways.

### A. Prayer

> *You can ask for anything in my name, and I will do it, so that the Son can bring glory to the Father. Yes, ask me for anything in my name, and I will do it! (John 14: 13,14, NLT)*

### B. Light and Life

We glorify Christ when our lives demonstrate our relationship with Christ as Lord. The <u>light</u> of our life is a witness of Christ. Though it may be silent, it glorifies our Father in heaven. **We are always a witness. Sometimes we speak!** On our jobs, in our homes, in school, in church or the community, we are to let our light shine by our attitudes, actions, and sometimes our words. The world needs to see that we are different, that we react differently than they do. Our attitudes are different in response to life. It includes faith and a trust in God that the world does not have. The world sees our good works and glorifies the Father in heaven (I Cor. 6:20).

> *Let your light so shine before men, that they may see your good works, and glorify your Father which is in heaven. (Matt 5:16, KJV)*

> *Having your conversation honest among the Gentiles: that, whereas they speak against you as evildoers, they may by your good works, which they shall behold, glorify God in the day of visitation. (1 Peter 2:12, KJV)*

### C. Praise and Worship

> *Whoever offers praise glorifies Me; and to him who orders his conduct aright I will show the salvation of God. (Psa. 50:23)*

> *... that you may with one mind and one mouth glorify the God and Father of our Lord Jesus Christ. (Rom. 15:6)*

### D. Bear Fruit

We glorify the Father when we **bear fruit**. We bear the Life of Christ in us. We demonstrate that we are disciples of Christ. Again, it is a silent witness. People see that our attitude is different in our responses to situations, our joy and peace are different, our faith is not shattered when situations arise, and we have joy in the midst of our lives even when we are having difficulty.

> *When you bear (produce) much fruit, My Father is honored and glorified, and you show and prove yourselves to be true followers of Mine. (John 15:8, AMP)*

> *... being filled with the fruits of righteousness which are by Jesus Christ, to the glory and praise of God. (Phil. 1:11)*

### E. Proclamation

We also glorify Christ when we make **proclamation of Him,** by speaking of Him to others, whether in a pulpit, on a streetcar, taxi, in the workplace, in school, or whenever we have the appropriate opportunity to share Christ. Sometimes, it may not be appropriate to witness verbally. Other times, we need to take advantage of the opportunities of sharing Christ ... even over the telephone. Jesus commanded His disciples to preach ... proclaim the Gospel. Paul said, **Woe is me if I preach not the Gospel** (II Cor. 5:14). There is a time to be silent, and there is a time to preach ... proclaim the "Good News" of the Gospel ... the Cross for the salvation of the lost. When we preach the Cross, we glorify Him (I Cor. 1:18; 2:2).

> *Whoever speaks, let him speak, as it were, the utterances of God; whoever serves, let him do so as by the strength which God supplies; so that in all things God may be glorified through Jesus Christ, to whom belongs the glory and dominion forever and ever. Amen. (I Pet. 4:11 NASB)*

## F. Miracles

Jesus said that we were to go to the whole world in His Name to **preach the Gospel, heal the sick, cast out devils**, and even **raise the dead** (Matt. 10:8). When that happens, it is a marvelous testimony of God's presence and glorifies Him. The New Testament testifies to that truth, as well as the myriad of miracles that are happening today (Acts 3:1-10; 9:36-43; 19:11-28).

> *Go home to your friends, and tell them what great things the Lord has done for you, and how He has had compassion on you. (Mark 5:19)*

## G. Love

**We demonstrate that we are disciples of Christ when we love one another.**

> *So now I am giving you a new commandment: Love each other. Just as I have loved you, you should love each other. Your love for one another will prove to the world that you are my disciples. (John 13:34,35, NLT)*

Why does a church fail to make missions primary? We are not talking primarily about money or going overseas (some cannot go, but can give). One can still have missions in prayer and intimacy with the Lord, who is Lord of missions! One reason is that we are not intimate with the Lord, who is the Lord of missions. He came to seek and to save that the world may enjoy the blessings afforded to them in Christ (Eph. 1:4-6,12,14).

Compassion and zeal for the glory of God are not separate. God-centered compassion weeps over the misery of people. The Church is to have one overriding passion of the One in whom all the fullness of God dwells, and who has reconciled all things unto Himself–Christ (Col. 1:19, 20)! Once our heart is centered on Him, we will be missionaries to one or to a multitude, here or abroad, in giving, in going, and always in prayer. When we have a passion for God, we will love what He loves, hate what He hates, do what He does, and say what He says ... all with limitations, of course (Eph. 6:7, 8). How do you know you love the sinner? When you love your heavenly Father, you know this stranger is created by Him, though separated from Him. You share Christ because of your love for Christ. Humanity does not deserve the love of God any more than any of us. We all deserve to be damned, but Jesus, the suffering Lamb of God, receives the reward of His suffering. Jesus paid it all!

A zeal for the glory of God then motivates world missions like nothing else, and keeps us motivated as we seek His glory, just as Christ came to glorify and magnify His Father. When God is our ultimate Goal, we can be motivated ... to do those things that Christ saw His Father do, say what He heard His Father say, and be obedient to His Father.

## SALVATION IS FOR GOD HIMSELF

See Ephesians 1:3-14 (Father, vv. 5,8; Son, vv. 7,11,12; Spirit, vv. 1:13,14). He also states in John 17:13,26 ... *that they might have my joy fulfilled in themselves ... that the love with which You loved Me may be in them, and I in them.* We have been *created for God's glory*, to be like God (Isa. 43:7; Eph. 1:3-7,11-14; Rom. 11:36).

> *Thou art worthy, O Lord, to receive glory and honor and power: for thou hast created all things, and for thy pleasure they are and were created. (Rev. 4:11, KJV)*

> *Even every one that is called by my name: for I have created him for my glory, I have formed him; yea, I have made him. (Isa 43:7)*

When countless millions of the redeemed fall on their faces before the Throne of God in worship of the Lamb forever and ever giving God glory, missions will be no more. It is necessary now until then. What a glorious end of missions! Until then, we move forward.

## WHAT IS GOD'S GLORY?

It speaks of the essential worth, beauty, and value of a person, created things, and the Creator. In the Hebrew the word is ***weight*** (substance, brilliance, beauty). It is alluded to in II Cor. 4:17: ... ***our lightness of affliction works out for us a far more exceeding weight of glory.***

*"To glorify"* means to recognize God's intrinsic worth and beauty and to praise and worship Him openly and truthfully. As previously stated, ***to magnify*** Him is to see Him bigger. We magnify God through praising His name and honoring His commandments (Psa. 86:12). Jesus also glorified His Father through His perfect obedience and His sacrificial death on our behalf (John 17:1). To give Him glory and honor is to recognize His universal sovereignty, His omnipotence, the I AM of the universe. He does not ask us what is right or wrong. He alone is just. What is loving? He is the most loving of all, for God is love. When one seeks the highest good, God consults with Himself ... for us and the world. All things were created to give praise and honor to God (II Cor. 4:5-7). Love for the lost must not be detached from our primary passion for the glory of God!

In Psalm 96, verses 2,3,7-9, God reveals His glory to all nations in order to receive glory from all of His creation in loving worship. Psa. 86:9: ***all nations ... shall come and worship ... and shall glorify Your Name.*** We have been saved from sin to worship. Abraham was blessed to be a blessing (Gen. 12:1-3; 14:18-20). Jesus is the ***brightness of the Father's glory*** (Heb. 1:3; John 1:14; 2:11). It was the desire of Christ that the disciples would share His glory. John 17:24: ... ***that they may behold My glory which You have given Me***. To the glory of God alone is the heart of true worship (Phil. 3:3; John 5:44). God chose His people *for His glory* (Eph. 1:4-6), ***our good works are to give glory to the Father*** (Matt. 5:16), our answered prayers are that God would be glorified (John 14:17). We do all things *for **His glory*** (I Cor. 10:31; 6:20). Revelation 4:11: **(Thou art worthy...);** Isa. 42: ... ***My Name ... My glory I will give to no other*** (Rom. 15:8,9; Psa. 96:1-4,7,10; 70:4; 72:18,19; Col. 1:15,16; Isaiah 40:28; 43:7). ***I have created him for my glory*** ... (Psa. 67; Isa. 48:9-11; I Cor. 1:31). ***The whole earth shall be filled with the knowledge of the glory of God*** (Hab. 2:14).

When a person is consumed with the glory of God with a passion of the worship of Him, he wants to make Him known in our world. Again, missions is not the goal, but the means of bringing people to worship God with a white hot passion. The ultimate passion of any missions work is to see God glorified. Worship, then, not only is the goal of missions, but the fuel of missions. It moves us to others ... our worship to God ... to see others worship also (Matt. 5:21,23; John 15:11; 17:13).

## CHRIST'S ULTIMATE GOAL: TO SHARE HIS GLORY WITH THE CHURCH!

> *And the glory which You gave Me I have given them, that they may be one just as We are one: I in them, and You in Me; that they may be made perfect in one, and that the world may know that You have sent Me, and have loved them as You have loved Me. (John 17:22,23)*

## FOR THE SAKE OF HIS NAME[3]

We are also motivated in missions by the Name of Christ. We want to see His Name honored, praised, worshiped, so that in the Day of the Lord He will be glorified ... a *chosen seed to bear My Name* (III John 6,7; Acts 9:15; Psa. 115:1) ... *unto Your Name give glory* (Psa. 67:3,4); ... *hallowed be Your Name ... Your Kingdom come* (Matt. 6:9,10).

God is committed to the glory of His great and holy Name. God will ultimately justify, prove, and defend His people and His Name in all the earth. In that day *every knee will bow and every tongue confess that Jesus Christ is Lord to the glory of the Father* (Phil. 2:9,10). His Name was given to Him by God Himself. It is a more excellent Name, higher than angels and principalities and power. He died on the Cross, rose again, and ascended on high to prove His excellence above all other names! Everlastingly reverenced! There will be a time when there will be no more missions conventions, offerings, travel to other countries, or to others next door ... no more sacrifices, no more martyrs or persecution, or the need of prayer for missionaries! What a glorious Day that will be! (John 16:23)

> *Therefore God also has highly exalted Him and given Him the name which is above every name, that at the name of Jesus every knee should bow, of those in heaven, and of those in earth, and of those under the earth, and that every tongue should confess that Jesus Christ is Lord, to the glory of God the Father. (Phil. 2:9-11)*

> *And I have declared to them Your name, and will declare it, that the love with which You loved Me may be in them, and I in them. (John 17:26)*

---

[3] See Appendix VIII.

Paul says that he endures suffering for the sake of His Name (Acts 9:16; 21:13; Phil. 3:8). Paul makes his mission statement clear: to see the name of Christ among all the nations.

> *Through Christ, God has given us the privilege and authority as apostles to tell Gentiles everywhere what God has done for them, so that they will believe and obey Him, bringing glory to His name. (Rom. 1:5, NLT)*

Paul saw the entire world in two categories: where Christ was named and where Christ was not yet named. His emphasis was to labor where Christ was not named (Rom. 15:20). Paul labored to glorify God by revealing Christ to the nations—getting Christ named. But Paul's highest zeal, the highest passion was that which was to come back to God *from the nations*—worship and praise to God Himself. Paul saw himself as a priest offering the sacrifice to God the offering of the Gentile saints sanctified by the Spirit (Rom. 15:15-17) to **glorify God** (Rom. 15:6). Thus, he was fulfilling the command of Christ to go **to all nations** (Acts 9:15,16; Col. 3:17; Matt. 19:29,30; Col. 3:17).

> *My ambition has always been to preach the Good News where the name of Christ has never been heard, rather than where a church has already been started by someone else. I have been following the plan spoken of in the Scriptures, where it says, "Those who have never been told about him will see, and those who have never heard of Him will understand." (Rom. 15:20,21, NLT)*

Missionaries go for the sake of the name and reputation of Jesus. God's goal is that His Son's name be exalted and honored among all the peoples of the world. For when the Son is honored, the Father is honored (Mark 9:37). When every knee bows at the name of Jesus, it will be **to the glory of God the Father** (Phil. 2:10,11). Therefore, God-centered missions exists and is motivated for the sake of the name of Jesus. We endure persecution and peril to see His Name honored ... to be praised ... to be worshiped, so that in the Day of the Lord *every knee shall bow and confess Jesus Christ as Lord, to the glory of God the Father* **(Psa. 115:1; Isa. 42:8; 48:11).**

> *Let the peoples praise You, O God; Let all the peoples praise You. Oh, let the nations be glad and sing for joy! (Psa. 67:3-4)*

> *Matt. 6:9,10: Hallowed be Your Name (Isa. 52:10,11 (Christ); John 14:13,14; 16:23,24).*

The ministry of sending is also a very high calling. They are fellow-workers with the missionaries on the field. It is crucial in all missionary endeavors for their prayer and support. With their participation, they will also reap the rewards of the seeds sown by missionaries.

> *Who have borne witness of your love before the church. If you send them forward on their journey in a manner worthy of God (in a manner that pleases God) you will do well, because they went forth for His name's sake, taking nothing from the Gentiles. For they are traveling for the Lord, and they accept nothing from people who are not believers. So we ourselves should support them so that we can be their partners as they teach the truth. (III John 6-8, NLT)*

## PREACHING IN HIS NAME

When we preach in His Name, we are giving Him honor. The man at the Gate Beautiful was healed in the Name of Jesus (Acts 3:6). His Name was preached and people were saved.

> *But so that it spreads no further among the people, let us severely threaten them, that from now on they speak to no man in this name. So they called them and commanded them not to speak at all nor teach in the name of Jesus. But Peter and John answered and said to them, "Whether it is right in the sight of God to listen to you more than to God, you judge." For we cannot but speak the things which we have seen and heard." (Acts 4:17-20)*

Paul spoke boldly in the Name of Jesus (with authority and authorization) (Acts 9:29).

> Jesus said (manifested presence of Christ): *"Where two or three are gathered together in My Name there am I in the midst of you."* (Matt. 18:20)

## SALVATION IS IN HIS NAME

> *Nor is there salvation in any other, for there is no other Name under heaven given among men by which we must be saved." (Acts 4:12)*

## HEALING AND MIRACLES ARE IN HIS NAME

Jesus said that signs would accompany them that believe in His Name (Acts 3:5,6,16; John 14:12-14).

> *And these signs will follow those who believe: In My name they will cast out demons; they will speak with new tongues; they will take up serpents; and if they drink anything deadly, it will by no means hurt them; they will lay hands on the sick, and they will recover. (Mark 16:17,18)*

> *They brought in the two disciples and demanded, "By what power, or in whose name, have you done this?" Then Peter, filled with the Holy Spirit, said to them, "Rulers and elders of our people, are we being questioned today because we've done a good deed for a crippled man? Do you want to know how he was healed? Let me clearly state to all of you and to all the people of Israel that he was healed by the powerful name of Jesus Christ the Nazarene, the man you crucified but whom God raised from the dead. (Acts 4:7-10, NLT)*

## AUTHORITY IN HIS NAME

Jesus has all authority and He has given us that authority in His Name. The Name stands for the Person of Christ, not a doctrine, but His power, His glory, and His authority (Matt. 28:18)!
  Casting out Devils—(see Mark 16:17; Luke 10:17-19; Acts 16:18)

> *I tell you the truth, anyone who believes in Me will do the same works I have done, and even greater works, because I am going to be with the Father. You can ask for anything in My name, and I will do it, so that the Son can bring glory to the Father. Yes, ask Me for anything in My name, and I will do it! (John 14:12-14, NLT)*

> *But the Lord said to him, Go, because this man is my chosen instrument to carry My Name before Gentiles and kings and the people of Israel. (Acts 9:15, NET)*

## <u>CONCLUDING NOTE</u>

Missions then has hope. We have Christ's own word. ... ***other sheep ... <u>they will listen</u> to My voice (John 10:16) ... all that the Father has given to me <u>shall</u> come to me (John 6:37) ... neither do I pray for these alone, but for*** *them also which shall believe on Me through their word (John 17:20).* Jesus said that our mission of preaching Christ will have success. What a promise! What an encouragement to us to go. There will be those who will hear and respond to the message, though not all. The mission of God will succeed! (John 17:26; Rev. 11:15; 21:3)

Let us be pleasure-seekers—making God our Pleasure. Let our pleasure be Him, not what He can give to us. We are to make Him our Delight, our ultimate Joy, our highest passionate Love, our reason for being to bring glory and honor to Him, and we will fulfill His desire for missions. When we do, the Scripture says, **Delight in the Lord and He shall give you the desires of your heart *(Psa. 37:4)*. ... in His presence is fullness of joy—pleasures forevermore *(Psa. 16:11)*.**

World evangelization is for God ... the priority goal of missions ... the glory of God—*declare His glory among the nations* (Psa. 96:3; Rev. 5:9)! God is most satisfied in us when we are most satisfied in Him. When I please Him, I not only make Him happy, but I am the happiest! **Be still and know [yada, be intimate] with Him** *(*as a husband with his wife, Psa. 46:10; Adam had a *yada* experience with his wife and they had a son (Gen. 4:1); **and I will be exalted in the nations, I will be exalted in the earth.** God seeks our praise and worship. When we please Him, we are most satisfied. He commands praise. He gets the glory and we get the pleasure!

---

"The chief end of man is to glorify God *by* enjoying Him forever."
—John Piper, *Desiring God*

---

Missions is to satisfy God Himself. I am the happiest when I make Him happy ...when I am intimate with Him, hear, and obey His voice. Again, be a pleasure-seeker. Let the Lord be your highest love, highest joy, and highest worship (Rom. 11:36). The <u>ultimate aim</u> is that we share His glory (John 17:4). We are the happiest when we make Him happy!

> *And they sang a new song, saying: "You are worthy to take the scroll, And to open its seals; For You were slain, And have redeemed us to God by Your blood out of every tribe and tongue and people and nation (ethnic group), And have made us kings and priests to our God; And we shall reign on the earth." (Rev. 5:9,10)*

> *All nations whom You have made shall come and worship before You, O Lord, and shall glorify Your name. For You are great, and do wondrous things; You alone are God. (Psa. 86:9,10)*
> See Also: Psa. 86:9,10; 96:1-3; 67:3,4; Mark 13:10; Rev. 7:9-12,14; 11:15; 19:6.

## **PEOPLE GROUPS**

These are distinct, homogeneous ethnic or racial groups within a single country speaking the same language (one single mother tongue). Estimates are that 11,487 large groups and 6,854 smaller groups have yet to be reached with the testimony of Christ (2.67 billion, 41%). That is 41.6% of the world's population of 6.3 billion+ people. That means 2.67 billion people have yet to hear the Gospel! (Joshua Project)

Matt. 24:14 – ***This Gospel is to be preached among all nations (ethnic groups) and then shall the end come*** (tribes, families [clans], language, people, and nations). II Pet. 3:9 – ***The Lord is not slack concerning His Promise, but is longsuffering, not willing that any should perish, but that all should come to repentance.***

Jesus Preaches in Galilee (Matt. 4:23-25; Mark 1:35-39; John 6:37,39)

> *Now when it was day, He departed and went into a deserted place. And the crowd sought Him and came to Him, and tried to keep Him from leaving them; but He said to them, "I must preach the kingdom of God to the other cities also." (Luke 4:42-43)*

> *I neither pray for these alone, but for them also which shall believe on Me through their word. (John 17:20)*

## **ILLUSTRATION**

Jim Elliott, missionary to the Auca Indians in Ecuador, was looking for people groups who were not yet worshipers of God. This is specific indication that the Gospel must be gotten to tribes who are not yet included in the singing hosts. "Hence, my burden for cultural groups is as yet untouched." Five missionaries were killed, because they left one ocean liner to save another! Yet these tribes have been reached with the Gospel, churches established, and reaching out to others. It happened because five missionaries gave their lives to reach them with the Gospel. The Auca tribe has since sent missionaries to other places of the world!

> "He is no fool who gives what he cannot keep
> to gain that which he cannot lose."
> —Jim Elliott

*The kingdoms of this world shall become the Kingdoms of our Lord and Christ. (Rev. 11:15)*

*And I heard a voice of a great multitude ... "Alleluia, for the Lord God omnipotent reigns!" (Rev. 19:6)*

*Praise the Lord, all you nations. Praise him, all you people of the earth. (Psa. 117:1, NLT)*

*When they found Him, they said to Him, "Everyone is looking for You." But He said to them, "Let us go into the next towns, that I may preach there also, because for this purpose I have come forth." (Mark 1:37-38, NLT)*

## <u>ILLUSTRATION</u>

Two ocean liners began to sink with many people on board who did not know how to swim. There were ten rescuers in two large boats. When they arrive, hundreds are sinking, some holding on to debris. Several hundred yards away, the same is taking place with the other ocean liner. There is lots of room in the rescue boats. The cry comes from both boats. Love cannot be the only motive for rescue, for distant souls are the same as those that are near. To row to the other ship, would deplete the energies of resources meaning less people saved. Love may refuse to leave the rescue effort. The issue is not to necessarily maximize the total number of individuals saved.

When Jesus spoke to the Samaritan woman, He left many who needed salvation. Why? He was doing the will of His Father, not counting heads as to the number of souls. Even the Samaritans, who had heard the revelation of Jesus from this woman at the well, begged Him not to leave them (John 4:40). God's desire is that there would be rescue operations from every people group of the world. It is possible to have rescue operations from every people group of the world—from BOTH ocean liners, even if the rescuers must leave a faithful ***"reached"*** people (first ocean liner) in order to labor among (and possibly less fruitful) ***"unreached"*** people (second ocean liner).

Jesus went to ***other cities*** (Luke 8:1;13:22; Mark 1:38; Luke 4:43). He went to Capernaum, Tyre and Sidon (Philistia), Decapolis, Syrophenician (Greek), Samaritans (considered "dogs" by Jews), a Roman Centurion, Caesarea-Philippi, Dalmatia, Gadara (demonized), Bethsaida, Nazareth, and Judea/Jordan. Today, some estimate that 80% of missionaries are working with people already "reached"—about 6% working with unreached people groups. The task of missions is not only to reach as many people as possible but to win individuals from all people groups of the world.

# PART TWO

# Chapter One

# Incarnation

God sent His Son wrapped in humanity, born of the Spirit. Thus, God totally identified Himself with mankind. **John 1:1,14** – *In the beginning was the Word and the Word was with God, and the Word was God... and the Word became flesh and dwelt among us (John 1:18)... no man has seen God at any time ... the Word has declared Him (John 10:17,18) ... I lay down my life voluntarily (John 1:1-3)... that which is from the beginning ... what we have heard, what we have seen, touched, look upon, and handled, the Word of Life* (Rom. 8:3; Eph. 2:15; Col. 1:22; Heb. 4:15; 7:26; II Cor. 8:9; John 10:17,18). He was the **Son of Man** completely identifying with all of mankind (Mark 10:45). (See Rom. 10:9-15; John 3:36; 14:6; I John 5:11,12; Matt.11:27; Heb. 4:15).

> "If Christ had been born by natural generation His blood would have been poisoned by the universal malady of sin and would have been absolutely valueless as an atonement for the sinful sons of men. It is an established physiological fact that the mother's blood is neither the source nor the supply of the blood of the unborn infant's veins. It is the contribution of the male, which leads to the development of the blood. Without that vital contribution, no blood could be produced because the female of herself does not produce the elements essential for the production of this new blood. Gray's *Anatomy*, a recognized medical authority, states, 'The fetal and maternal blood-currents do not intermingle, being separated from each other by the delicate walls of the villi.'" (*Christian Foundations*, Richard Paisley, p. 56)

*By this you know the Spirit of God: Every spirit that confesses that Jesus Christ has come in the flesh is of God, and every spirit that does not confess that Jesus Christ has come in the flesh is not of God. And this is the spirit of the Antichrist, which you have heard was coming, and is now already in the world. (1 John 4:2,3)*

*... a body You have prepared Him. ... God needed a body of sacrifice as a requirement to fulfill the OT Law. (Heb. 10:5,10)*

## REVEAL HIS FATHER[4]

Jesus came in human form to reveal and glorify His Father, to make Him Precious. Jesus said that when you see Me, you see my Father. I give My Father the highest level of honor and praise—nothing or no one is superior!

Jesus is more than a powerful Force, an unknown, or a Supreme Being! He was and is **_God in the flesh_**! He spoke like God. He acted like God. He died like God. He rose again like God. He ascended into heaven like God. He was God! He is God. He will ever be God! John tells us one criterion for discerning the Spirit of God.

## IDENTIFICATION WITH MANKIND (SELF-EMPTYING OF DEITY TO BE FULLY MAN)

Jesus came self-emptying of deity to be fully human as God ... to identify with the lowest of humanity. According to Isaiah 53:2, Jesus was not handsome —***There was nothing beautiful or majestic about his appearance, nothing to attract us to him.*** He came from Nazareth, a city that had a very bad reputation (John 1:46). He was born in a dirty, smelly stable, not in a sanitized hospital room. Some would say that He was an illegitimate child, born out of wedlock (John 8:41). Yes, Jesus fully identified with us without losing His identity. He was given a very common name, not one appropriate for a king (Joshua, Jehovah is Salvation). He submitted Himself to His parents and to water baptism. He identified with tax collectors and sinners (Luke 15:1, 2), and on the Cross He hung between two thieves (Luke 23:32,33) ... a true servant (Phil. 2:5-9). He identified with every class—the religious, the political, lepers and the sick, children, the blind, and the demon possessed. He allowed a woman of ill repute to anoint His head with oil—an act totally abominable to the religious leaders. He touched the lepers, cast the devils

---

[4] John 1:14, 18; 14:6, 7; Heb. 1:3; John 10:30

out of a naked man in Gadara. He was mocked and ridiculed in His life and rejected by the disciples. He who fed the multitude came to the point of dependence upon others for sustenance (John 1:14; Luke 8:3,4; 10:38). He had no place to lay His head (Matt. 8:20). He accepted the help of others. He needed a colt to ride upon, *because He had need of* him (Luke 19;30,31). Though He was rich, *He became poor for our sake, that through His poverty we might be made rich (II Cor. 8:9)*. The Creator, the Almighty, and the I AM of the universe lived upon the alms of others. He became One in need of help (II Cor. 5:20, 21; Isa. 40:5)!

Christ loved the rich young ruler, but refused to compromise the message He gave to him. He told him to sell all that he had and give to the poor. The young ruler refused and left Him. The Bible says that Jesus *loved him* (Matt. 10:18-22). He was truly the Man of all seasons. He owned no more than what He carried. He did not impress the economic world (Matt. 6:19-21). Jesus, who, as God, was the agent of creation, became a humble member of the humanity He created (Col. 1:16). This Man, Christ Jesus, is the One Whom we love and serve with joy (I Tim. 2:5,6; Heb. 10:5-7,10; Isa. 53:4-6).

He came to be a servant (Phil. 2:2-11), to wash feet, not to have crowns put on His head! He knew hunger (Matt. 4:2), thirst (John 19:28), and exhaustion (John 14:6). He experienced sorrow (Mark 9:5), grieving of people (Mark 9:5), joy (Luke 10:21), and compassion (Matt. 9:36-38; Luke 7:13; 15:20). He knows what we are going through in life. The announcement of His birth was given to shepherds who were known to steal sheep and lands. They had lost their respect since the time of David. They were not the best messengers to carry the news of the birth of a King! He experienced rejection (Luke 22:31-34 – Peter).

> *Let this mind be in you which was also in Christ Jesus, who, being in the form of God, did not consider it robbery to be equal with God, but made Himself of no reputation, taking the form of a bondservant, and coming in the likeness of men. And being found in appearance as a man, He humbled Himself and became obedient to the point of death, even the death of the cross. (Phil 2:5-8)*

> *Forasmuch then as the children are partakers of flesh and blood, he also himself likewise took part of the same; that through death he might destroy him that had the power of death, that is, the devil. (Heb. 2:14, KJV)*

> *... touched with the feelings of our infirmities.... This High Priest of ours understands our weaknesses, for he faced all of the same testings we do, yet he did not sin. (Heb. 4:15 NLT)*

He came not only to deliver a message, He *was* the Message! His life was exactly what His words were. The living Word became flesh and we beheld His glory. He came as the good Shepherd to give His life a ransom for the sheep. His life was exactly what His words were. He was ***moved with compassion*** to heal the leper (Mark 1:41). He was ***moved with compassion*** again and fed the multitude (Mark 8:2). Again, when He saw the multitude, His inner bowels were ***moved with compassion*** when He saw them ***as sheep not having a shepherd*** (Matt. 9:36-38; Luke 7:13; 15:20). He relates to every class—the religious, political leaders, lepers, children, the blind, the demon possessed, men as well as women, the helpless, the hungry, and the homeless with ***no place to lay His head*** (Luke 9:58). He became sin that He might redeem sinners.

He came to give His life a ransom. To follow Christ as our Missionary Example, we are to fully identify with all people as much as possible in their culture, yet without compromise. God used the people of Israel to be the Covenant People (incarnation) to demonstrate and proclaim the message of Redemption to the world.

> *For He made Him who knew no sin to be sin for us, that we might become the righteousness of God in Him. (II Cor. 5:21)*

## APPLICATION: SERVANTHOOD

The servant of Christ is not greater than His Lord (John 13:16). He came to identify with those He came to save. As Jesus came to serve and not be served (Mark 10:45), we who are His followers are to love one another with brotherly affection and outdo one another showing honor by serving (Rom. 12:10; Luke 22:27). The followers of Jesus by love serve one another with humility (Gal. 5:13; Luke 14:11). Whoever wants to be first and the greatest among you, must be a slave of all (Mark 10:44; Matt. 10:44; 23:27). Greatness is being a servant to Christ and to others. To follow Christ in His Incarnation as our Model and our mission to the world, we must have compassion for the lost (Matt. 9:36), become all things to all men for the sake of the Gospel (I Cor. 9:22b), and servant of all (Mark 9:23). There is a cost of serving and washing dirty feet. One must lay aside the garments of pride and position. The true test of love is not how we relate to the lovely, the saints, and the scholars, but to sinners, tax collectors, the unlovely and unwanted in our world. To model Jesus and love and serve others is to do for that person as if He were in your place. To follow Jesus is to lead with a towel of servanthood, not the title of position. We follow Jesus' example as His servants!

> *Verily, verily, I say unto you, the servant is not greater than his lord; neither he that is sent greater than he that sent him. If ye know these things, happy are ye if ye do them. (John 13:16,17, KJV)*

That is the challenge. Will people still see me as a leader when I wash feet? Will they still respect me dressed as a servant and serving with a towel? If you are following the world's system, probably not. But, if Jesus is your Model, follow Him, get His approval, and be blessed by Him. Who you are is not dependent upon what you do, but who God has destined you to be … what He has called you to be—a son or daughter of the Almighty, the everlasting Father! How do we wash one another's feet? How do we serve one another?

> *Be good friends who love deeply; practice playing second fiddle. (Rom. 12:10, MSG)*

> *Therefore, however you want people to treat you, so treat them, for this is the Law and the Prophets. (Matt. 7:12, NASB)*

The follower of Jesus by love serves others with humility (Galatians 5:13). **For everyone who tries to honor himself shall be humbled; and he who humbles himself shall be honored** (Luke 14:11, NLT). In washing the feet of the disciples, Christ gave an example of love, for this is the nature of love—to serve and to be submissive to one another.

> *Whoever wants to be a leader among you must be your servant, and whoever wants to be first among you must be the slave of everyone else. For even the Son of Man came not to be served but to serve others and to give his life as a ransom for many. (Mark 10:43-45, NLT)*

Greatness is being a servant to Christ and to others. To follow Christ in His Incarnation and our mission to the world, we must have compassion for the lost (Matt. 9:36), become all things to all men for the sake of the Gospel (I Cor. 9:22b), and to be the servant of all. There is a cost to serving and washing dirty feet. One must lay aside the garments of pride and also position. The true test of love is not only how we relate to the lovely, the saints and scholars, but to sinners, the lower caste of society, tax collectors, and the unlovely and unwanted in our world. To follow Jesus is to lead with a towel of servanthood, not the title of position. It is making Jesus Lord of our lives in all areas. We follow Jesus' example as His servants! By washing the disciples' feet, He did not cease being the Lord, the Son of God. What He did was not what defined who He was! Neither will we lose our identity of who we are in Christ and His call in our lives when we serve, even without recognition.

Servanthood leadership is meekness not weakness ... not authoritarian, but with authority! It is serving with towels not titles. Servant-leaders follow Jesus rather than seek a position. They humble themselves and wait for God to exalt them, if He does. Our lives become our message to the people as well as our words.

> *Who is greater, the one who reclines at the table (the master), or the one who serves? Is it not the one who reclines at the table? But I am in your midst as One who serves. (Luke 22:27)*

> *I have been crucified with Christ; it is no longer I who live, but Christ lives in me; and the life which I now live in the flesh I live by faith in the Son of God, who loved me and gave Himself for me. (Gal. 2:20)*

> *For those who exalt themselves will be humbled, and those who humble themselves will be exalted. (Luke 14:11, NLT)*

He came to give His life a ransom. He came to serve, not to be served. To follow Christ as our Missionary Example, we are to fully identify with all people as much as possible in their culture, yet without compromise. God used the people of Israel to be the Covenant People (incarnation) to demonstrate and proclaim the message of Redemption to the world.

**I believe in reincarnation.** God again coming in human flesh to reveal Himself to the world through His Church. This is the great Mystery—*Christ in us, the Hope of Glory* (Col. 1:27). Jesus said that He would be *in* us as a witness so that the world would know Christ's mission (John 17:23). The Church is filled with **the fullness of God** (Eph. 1:23). We are the Body of Christ (Eph. 4:12-16), the **temple of God** (I Cor. 3:16). Christ is reincarnated in His Church! The Church is the visible representation of Christ on earth. What the world sees is Christ in His Church, both faltering and triumphant!

Are there any that are living the life of Christ? Of course! Mother Teresa and Hudson Taylor are famous examples of those who have lived out the life of Christ in their lives. There are those serving victims of the AIDS epidemic in Africa, where I was last year. The slums, the drug addicts, those in the high places in government, in our Congress, judges, and all levels of society are being served by Christ-followers. We identify! We are living out Christ in our lives. Christ is IN us! (See Addendum I)

**Question: *Do you want to be great?*** To be a disciple of Christ and to follow Him as the Model Missionary, we follow Him not from a platform of power and privilege but sacrificial servanthood. To be a foot-washer, one must deny oneself, ***preferring one another*** over oneself (Rom. 12:10), and serve with humility of spirit, without recognition or even thanks! Our attitude should be the same as that of Christ ... (Phil. 2:5; 4:12,13; Gal. 5:13-16).

> *Verily, verily, I say unto you, the servant is not greater than his Lord; neither he that is sent greater than he that sent him. If ye know these things, happy are ye if ye do them. (John 13:16,17 KJV)*
>
> *For those who exalt themselves will be humbled, and those who humble themselves will be exalted. (Luke 14:11)*
>
> *... and whoever wants to be first among you must be the slave of everyone else. For even the Son of Man came not to be served but to serve others and to give his life as a ransom for many. (Mark 10:44,45 NLT)*

So the question needs to be asked: Who is the greatest in the Kingdom of God? When James and John wanted a special place in Christ's Kingdom, and when the other disciples heard their request, Jesus responded by saying that whoever wants to be your servant would be the greatest. We are not greater than our Lord.

When we are truly servants, there are much fewer barriers to outreach in our community. We have met Philippine workers around the world serving as nannies with college degrees that they might not only work, but witness of Christ. Some were removed from Saudi Arabia because of their witness of Christ. We are Christ's servants. We are not greater than our Lord. Our life becomes our message to people. We find service as our means of following Christ. Your life becomes your message to the people and you also speak.

How do we know if we have a servant's heart? When people treat us as a servant, what is our reaction? The Spirit of God gives us the right attitude. He can change us to become not only a servant outwardly, but one inwardly from the heart. Our life becomes our message to the people and sometimes you speak. When we serve with a servant heart, we do not care much about who gets the credit, but that God gets the glory!

One of the greatest needs in the Church today is for leaders and pastors who serve with humility—servant-leaders, not dictators, or power-hungry. Pride is the root of all sin. God has called us to missions with a servant heart for *God resists the proud, but gives grace to the humble* **(James 4:6).** He gives us grace to love and serve Him and others, not out of duty, but of delight. Luke 14:11 — *"For whoever exalts himself will be humbled, and he who humbles himself will be exalted."* Even Jesus, who for the *JOY* set before Him endured the Cross. Paul says, *"I have become all things to all people, that by all means I might save some"* **(I Cor. 9:22).**

If we are going to follow Jesus in mission, He told us **to** *come unto Me, all ye that labor and are heavy laden ... take My yoke upon you and learn of Me: for I am meek and lowly... and you shall find rest for your souls* **(Matt. 11:28, 29, NKJV).** One of the greatest needs in the Church today is that we need leaders who serve with humility, servant-leaders, not dictators, or power hungry. Pride is the root of all sin. God has called us to missions with a servant heart for *God resists the proud, but gives grace to the humble (James 4:6).* He gives us grace to love and serve Him and others, not out of duty, but of delight. Luke 14:11 — **For whoever exalts himself will be humbled, and he who humbles himself will be exalted.** Even Jesus, who for the *JOY* set before Him endured the Cross. Paul says, *I have become all things to all people, that by all means I might save some (I Cor. 9:22,* **ESV).** Servant-leaders follow Jesus rather than seek a position. They humble themselves and wait for God to exalt them, if He does.

> *For we do not preach ourselves, but Jesus Christ as Lord, and ourselves as your servants for Jesus' sake. For God, who said, Let light shine out of darkness, made his light shine in our hearts to give us the light of the knowledge of the glory of God in the face of Christ. But we have this treasure in earthen vessels, that the excellence of the power may be of God and not of us. (II Cor. 4:5-10)*

**Note**: When one wanted to hide a treasure, they would often put the treasure in a clay pot knowing that no one would look into a refuse pot for anything of value!

> *If you only look at us, you might well miss the brightness. We carry this precious Message around in the unadorned clay pots of our ordinary*

> *lives. That's to prevent anyone from confusing God's incomparable power with us. (II Cor. 4:7, MSG)*

We are the Body of Christ (John 14:17,28; 17:20). We have been gifted by Christ to represent Him on earth as His servants, not dictators (I Cor. 12:12-17; Eph. 4:4-12). In I Corinthians 3:16 it says that *we are the* **Temple of God**. In Ephesians 2:22 it says that we are the **habitation of God**. The Church is the visible representation of Christ on earth. What the world sees in Christ is His Church, faltering and triumphant!

Christ is reincarnated through His Church ... the Life of Christ. When you hold the hand of the dying, comfort the sick, sit quietly in a waiting room after an operation, help the elderly and the depressed ... when you sit with a drug addict going through withdrawals ... when you share the Gospel, give godly counsel to those distressed by broken homes and marriages ... when you help the needy, clothe the naked, give a cup of cold water in His Name ... when you feed the hungry and visit the prisoner ... when you stand for truth and righteousness with the minority ... when you weep with those who weep and rejoice with those who rejoice ... when you witness of Christ, knock on doors, preach, heal and manifest His Name ... it is Christ *IN* you the *HOPE of Glory*. We are *IN* Christ (Col. 2:10). We are on His mission, not our own. We represent Him on the earth ... either good or bad.

We are *ambassadors* for Christ (II Cor. 5:20,21). We represent another country from another Kingdom and from another King. Our attitude is to be that of the King, Christ Jesus. We carry this **treasure** in *unadorned clay pots ... frail and feeble that the this extraordinary power will be known to be of God and not of us.* Paul said that *though I am free and belong to no man, I make myself a slave to everyone, to win as many as possible* (II Cor. 4:5-15).

Some clay pots were used to hide treasures, because no thief would look for a treasure in them. The glory of God shines, not because of the worth of the vessel, but because He is!

## **ILLUSTRATION**

The principle of "contextualization," or of making the Gospel as relevant to a given ethnic people as possible, without compromising the biblical truth, is illustrated by Paul's issue with circumcision. Paul had Timothy, who had a Jewish mother, circumcised in order to be found acceptable to the Jews (Acts 16:3). However, accommodation to a people halts (stops), if it is in conflict with Scripture. Paul refused to circumcise Titus, so that it would not give the message that a Christian had to first observe the Law (Gal. 2:2-5). Normally, circumcision is not an issue (I Cor. 7:18,19). Yet, it was Paul who illustrates this truth (Phil. 2:5-7).

> *For though I am free from all men, I have made myself a servant to all, that I might win the more; and to the Jews I became as a Jew, that I might win Jews; to those who are under the law, as under the law, that I might win those who are under the law; to those who are without law, as without law (not being without law toward God, but under law toward Christ), that I might win those who are without law; to the weak I became as weak, that I might win the weak. I have become all things to all men, that I might by all means save some. Now this I do for the gospel's sake, that I may be partaker of it with you. (I Cor. 9:19-23)*

## ILLUSTRATION

Henri J. M. Nouwen wrote *In the Name of Jesus*. He was a Jesuit priest, wrote several large theological books, graduated from seminary with several degrees, and taught in seminaries and universities in America and abroad. He chose to be a chaplain to a home for autistics (those who fail to use language properly and react to surroundings differently). He became a servant, not with his degrees or titles, but with a towel and a servant heart of Christ to serve these unfortunate people. That is the reincarnation of Christ!

Again, we are the incarnation of Christ when we pray in His Name, pleading His cause for others. When we go around the world or to our next door neighbor to preach the Gospel, or share the love of God and witness of Christ on our jobs or school ... whether we preach to crowds or to one (as Jesus did so many times) ... when we are silent, but speak volumes with our life ... it is Christ *IN* you! We are the **Incarnation of Christ** (see Addendum I). We are committed as the Body of Christ to serve Christ and to serve <u>**one another**</u> (Addendum V).

# Chapter Two

# The Purpose of His Coming

## A. REDEMPTION[5]

> ... *for the Son of Man has come to seek and to save that which was lost.* (Luke 19:10)

> *I am the Light of the world.* (John 8:12)

> *Behold the Lamb of God which takes away the sins of the world.* (John 1:29)

Jesus came to restore what Adam had lost in his sin, the image of God. Jesus came to seek and to save the lost. He came to give His life a ransom (Matt. 20:28). Jesus came to establish His church from every people group in the world that would be capable of multiplying congregations of that entire people group in the fellowship of the church worldwide.

Christ ***became sin for us ... that we might be the Righteousness of God*** (II Cor. 5:21). He came to redeem sinners (I Cor. 1:30; Isa. 53:4-6, 9-12; Rom. 8:3). He came ***to give His life a ransom*** (Matt. 20:28) ... deliver from demonic powers (Matt. 14:14), and feed the multitude (Mark 8:2). He was also ***moved with compassion*** in bringing healing (Mark 1:41, the leper cleansed). He ***went about doing good*** (Acts 10:38), secondary to redemption. He so identified with us so that He was and is ***touched with the feelings of our infirmities*** (Heb. 4:15). He came and did all of this, but He came primarily for redemption of mankind.

Since Jesus came ***to seek and to save the lost*** (Luke 19:10), it is our mandate to follow His model and make the winning of the lost our priority (Matt. 20:28; Rom. 10:9-15; John 3:36; 14:6; I John 5:11,12; Matt. 11:27).

---

[5] John 1:1,29; 3:16,17; 10:11 (I am the good Shepherd ... the good Shepherd gives His life for the sheep); 12:32 (If I be lifted up I will draw all men to Me).

His goal was to establish a community of the King within every people group in the world capable of multiplying congregations of that entire people group into a fellowship of the Church worldwide. God is ***not willing that any should perish...but that all should come to repentance*** (II Pet. 3:9; I Cor. 1:30,31; Rom. 3:24,25; II Cor. 5:21).

> *In Him we have redemption through His blood, the forgiveness of sins, according to the riches of His grace... (Eph. 1:7)*

> *He himself is the sacrifice that atones for our sins—and not only our sins but the sins of all the world. (I John 2:2, NLT)*

## JESUS AND ETERNAL LIFE

The Scripture makes it very clear that one can only have eternal life through Jesus Christ, the reason why He came (Isa. 53:4-6).

> *But as many as received Him, to them He gave the right to become children of God, to those who believe in His name ... (John 1:12)*

> *Jesus answered and said to him, "Most assuredly, I say to you, unless one is born again, he cannot see the kingdom of God." (John 3:3)*

> *And this is what God has testified: He has given us eternal life, and this life is in his Son. Whoever has the Son has life; whoever does not have God's Son does not have life. (I John 5:11,12, NLT)*

## B. <u>TO DESTROY THE WORKS OF THE DEVIL</u>

Jesus came to destroy the works of the devil.

> *For this purpose the Son of God was manifested, that He might destroy the works of the devil. (I John 3:8)*

> *And they overcame him by the blood of the Lamb and by the word of their testimony, and they did not love their lives to the death. (Rev. 12:11)*

We are to preach the Gospel, heal the sick, and cast out devils. There is no bondage that Jesus has not come to liberate. No sin or habit that cannot be conquered. No stronghold that Satan has on us that Christ has not come to destroy and liberate. He has come to set us free from Satan's stranglehold, from sin's stronghold. We are not bound to our past. We have been liberated by Christ. Christ disarmed the principalities and powers on the Cross for we **wrestle not against flesh and blood ...** (Eph. 6:12; II Cor.).

## C. <u>TO SATISFY THE LOVE OF GOD</u>

What is the heart of God in missions? The great heart of God must be satisfied—a deep yearning that must be fulfilled. How can world missions satisfy the heart of God? How can His Name be justified and praised?

We all know John 3:16: *For God <u>SO</u> loved the world...* Romans 5:8— *But God demonstrates His own love toward us, in that while we were still sinners, Christ died for us.* God loves the world with an intense passion. God demonstrated His love for His creation with a promise of redemption in speaking to Satan. Genesis 3:15—*I will put enmity between you and the woman ... between your offspring and her offspring ... he shall bruise (Cross and the Resurrection) your head and you shall bruise his heel (Cross)*, even before providing a sacrifice for Adam and Eve (Gen. 3:21). These were all acts of grace, all undeserving. We are not told that they asked for it! God <u>SO</u> loved the world, yes, even Adam and Eve. The good and the ugly. Those who are religious and those who are ungodly. God <u>SO</u> loved the world! He also loved sinners, rebellious, religious, hypocrites, atheists, homosexuals, terrorists, and the proud. If we are to follow Christ as His Example in world missions, we are to ask Him for that kind of love for the lost, a passion for those who need a Savior! Many are doing it in faraway places, in underground churches, in caves, unknown to man, but well known to God—for God <u>SO</u> loved the world. I read recently of a group of believers having "**church**" lying down in a rice field. Since the rice plants were so high, they were hidden from the authorities. The church meets in small villages, in the jungles of South America and Africa, in the ghettos and in major cities—for God <u>SO</u> loved the world. From the slums in major cities in India (where I have been), others around the world to the rural churches in Africa (where I have been)—for God <u>SO</u> loved the world. Rescuing children sold into slavery of human trafficking, and open sexual partners, loving them as Christ loved them, thus satisfying the heart of God. God rejoices that His Son did not die in vain (Isa. 53:11).

Does the world need to know the passionate love of God? Of course! When our love for God and the world is passionate, we are fulfilling the desire of God, whether there is a positive response or not. Jesus did not have all respond to His love, yet He continued to love. We make Him joyous. He receives praise and worship. Love rescues!

In Luke 15, the picture is seen in the parable of the shepherd who left the ninety and nine to seek the one **lost sheep.** *Rejoice with me; for I have found my sheep which was lost.*

Then there is the parable of the **lost coin** in Luke 15. The woman lights a lamp and sweeps the house and looks carefully, until she finds it. When she finds it, she summons her friends saying, *Rejoice with me, for I have found the silver coin which I had lost.*

Luke 15 continues with the parable of the **lost son**. The love of the Father is shown when the son returns to his father and there is great rejoicing. The father kisses him while the son is still in his filth, clothes him with new robes, puts new sandals on him, and has a party. *My son was lost, but now is found.* There is also joy in heaven when the son comes home. What keeps the son home? The delight of the Father in the son. Now, that is extraordinary grace!

We can make a party in heaven when we share Christ and one sinner repents. There is joy in heaven when that happens. That is the **LOVE** of God!

*Greater love has no one than this, than to lay down one's life for his friends. (John 15:13, NLT)*

*But God demonstrates His own love toward us, in that while we were still sinners, Christ died for us. (Rom 5:8, NLT)*

*But God, who is rich in mercy because of His great love with which He loved us, even when we were dead in trespasses, made us alive together with Christ (by grace you have been saved). (Eph. 2:4, NLT)*

One of my father's favorite verses is found in Romans 8:32—*He who did not spare His own Son, but delivered Him up for us all, how shall He not with Him also freely give us all things?* Most religions do not know the love of God, but only a god of wrath and rules.

Again, this constraining love to Christ demands missions. God's love for the world and our love for Him desires and demands fulfillment. The world needs to know the love of God where there **will be** *joy in the presence of the angels!* God rejoices that His Son did not die in vain. *His soul shall be satisfied* (Isa. 53:11). Millions have come to Christ, because of the love of God and the obedience of His Son.

Paul says that the love of Christ compels, controls and urges him in missions. It was his highest motivation for mission—God, not man!

> For the love of Christ compels us, because we judge thus: that if One died for all, then all died; and He died for all, that those who live should live no longer for themselves, but for Him who died for them and rose again. (II Cor. 5:14)

## D. TO SATISFY THE HOLINESS OF GOD

World missions is more than to satisfy the love of God. God demands holiness for entrance into heaven, for God holy—**_holiness, without which no man shall see the Lord_** *(Heb. 12:14)*. If there will be no sin in heaven, and since we all have sinned, then, unless something happens, there will be no one in heaven (Matt. 25:46; Mark 9:44,46,48; Luke 16:26; John 5:29)! Yet, the Bible says that there will be multitudes of the redeemed in heaven with the Lord; heaven will be full! He could save all men without repentance and faith. Yet, Hebrews 1:9 states, **_"You have loved righteousness and hated lawlessness..."_** Paul states, **_Knowing, therefore, the terror of the Lord, we persuade men (II Cor. 5:11)_**. He also said, **_Woe is me if I preach not the Gospel..._**. Holiness and love cannot be separated. His just wrath is an expression of His holy love. To redeem the world, He must satisfy His own character.

---

> If God is only loving, why not all in heaven?
> If God is only holy, we all deserve hell!

---

Isaiah saw his own uncleanness. He also saw the Lord, high and lifted up. (Isa. 6:5). God commissioned him to world evangelization only after Isaiah saw his own uncleanness and God's holiness. His lips were touched by an angel from heaven. He then received his commission from God Himself. **_There is no one holy like the Lord_** (Isa. 6:1-13; I Sam. 2:2). What was the condition of man that demanded such a price as the cross to satisfy the demands of God's holiness?

> *Then I heard the Lord asking, "Whom should I send as a messenger to this people? Who will go for us?" I said, "Here I am. Send me." (Isa. 65:1-10, NLT)*

When Adam sinned, who was the offended party, Adam or God? Let us see what the Bible says about the condition of man. So often we think of "poor humanity." God's view is that mankind has rebelled against God with wicked hearts and minds, rejected the truth, proudly shook its fist at God, declared their own independence, and made God after their own image. God's view is that the monstrous sin of man deserves judgment! The Bible is very clear about the condition of man (Rom. 1:18-31). Man is guilty ... lost and damned without hope. To reject God's love is to receive His wrath (John 3:36; Eph. 2:1-3; 4:18,19).

> *For all have sinned and come short of the glory of God ... and the wages of sin is death, but the gift of God is eternal life through Jesus Christ. (Rom. 3:23; 6:23)*

> *... be ye holy for I am holy. (I Pet. 1:16, KJV)*

> *Blessed are the pure in heart: for they (only) shall see God. (Matt. 5:8, KJV)*

> *Pursue peace with all people, and holiness, without which no one will see the Lord. (Heb. 12:14)*

Paul, in chapters 1-3 of Romans, speaks clearly that man is guilty. God shows His anger, His hatred of sin from heaven. In chapter 1, mankind has rejected God's revelation of His existence to mankind. Mankind became foolish, the body perverted, unthankful, refusing to worship their Creator. Their mind became corrupted. Claiming to be wise they became fools. They engaged in all sorts of sexual immorality and wickedness. They became wicked in their thoughts and deeds. When the world knew God, they rejected Him. Men became worshipers of idols that resembled mere people, birds, animals, and snakes, etc. God gave them up to fulfill their own lusts with pride, perversion, and wickedness of all sorts. They embraced their wicked deeds and they endorsed those who practiced them. *"**God gave them up** ... (v.24) ... **God gave them up** ...(v. 26) ... **God gave them up** ... (v. 28)."*

## **THE VERDICT: GUILTY!**

In chapter 2 of Romans, Paul describes God's dealing with three kinds of people. Each is charged with high treason against God. The moral person is also guilty, for he has not kept the law perfectly. He claims not to be as bad as others. He was condemning those that do not have his understanding, yet was doing the same things in his actions. He is to the object of God's terrible wrath and also experiences sorrow and suffering (2:9-11). These are the Sadducees and Pharisees of Jesus day. Jesus called them *children of the devil* (Matthew 23:13).

The religious Jew says that he knew the law of God and taught courses in religion. God says, "You don't practice what you preach." Because of your hypocrisy, you dishonor God's holy name among the Gentiles. You are breaking all of God's laws. The penalty and wages of sin is death. God judges righteously. Jesus called the Pharisees and the Sadducees *fools, hypocrites, blind guides, full of iniquity, serpents, a generation of vipers,* and *of your father the devil* (Matt. 23:13; John 8:34).

> You are of your father the devil, and the desires of your father you want to do. He was a murderer from the beginning, and does not stand in the truth, because there is no truth in him; when he speaks a lie, he speaks from his own resources, for he is a liar and the father of it. But because I tell the truth, you do not believe Me. (John 8:44,45)

## **THE VERDICT: GUILTY!**

The pagan person believes that he should be acquitted (found not guilty) because of ignorance. God says, "You have the two witnesses of conscience and nature." You have rejected both of them. You have refused to worship the Creator and you have rejected your conscience as to what is right and wrong. Therefore, you will be judged by these and not by the written Law.

The divine wrath upon the unbelieving world is just. They have rebelled against clear revelation with wicked hearts and minds, rejected the truth, proudly shook their fist at God, declared their own independence, and made God after their own image. Man has rejected the revelation of creation and conscience. Even when Jesus was here on earth, many rejected Him. They crucified Him. To reject God's love is to receive His wrath. Does that sound too harsh? Here is what our loving God says (II Thess. 1:8,9; John 3:36; Rom. 1:18; Rev. 21:8):

> The Lord is righteous in all his ways, and holy in all his works. (Psa. 145:17)

> He who believes in the Son has everlasting life; and he who does not believe the Son shall not see life, but the wrath of God abides on him. (John 3:36)

> And this is the condemnation, that the light has come into the world, men loved darkness rather than light, because their deeds were evil. For everyone practicing evil hates the light and does not come to the light, lest his deeds should be exposed. But he who does the truth comes to the light, that his deeds may be clearly seen, that they have been done in God. (John 3:19-21)

*Their minds are full of darkness; they wander far from the life God gives because they have closed their minds and hardened their hearts against him. They have no sense of shame. They live for lustful pleasure and eagerly practice every kind of impurity. (Eph. 4:18,19, NLT)*

*Knowing, therefore, the terror of the Lord, we persuade men; but we are well known to God, and I also trust are well known in your consciences. (II Cor. 5:11)*

## THE VERDICT

God is in a dilemma! He is so loving, He wants everyone to be with Him in heaven. He is so holy, everyone deserves hell, including you and me! However, holiness and love cannot be separated. He is God. His just wrath is an expression of His holy love. To redeem the world He must satisfy His own character of being both merciful and just. Otherwise, He would be imperfect and, therefore, not God! If God is all love and not light, there is no need for Christian mission. He could save all men without repentance and faith (I John 4:16). Hebrews 1:9 states, **You have loved righteousness and hated lawlessness...** Paul states, **Knowing, therefore, the terror of the Lord, we persuade men ... (II Cor. 5:11).** He also said, **Woe is me if I preach not the Gospel ...(I Cor. 9:16).** God is Light. **God is light and in Him is no darkness ...** (I John 1:5). Christ **loves righteousness and hates iniquity** (Heb. 1:9).

Paul goes further in saying, **knowing the terror of the Lord, we persuade men!** (II Cor. 5:11)

*God is love. (I John 4:16)*

*The devil, who deceived them, was cast into the lake of fire and brimstone where the beast and the false prophet are. And they will be tormented day and night forever and ever. (Rev. 20:10)*

*But the cowardly, unbelieving, abominable, murderers, sexually immoral, sorcerers, idolaters, and all liars shall have their part in the lake which burns with fire and brimstone, which is the second death. (Rev. 21:8)*

## WHAT IS GOD'S ANSWER? THE CROSS!

Today, too often, we have guiltless evangelism, user-friendly, seeker-sensitive, and counseling that bypasses the cross of repentance, faith, and true conversion. So often, we want to put everyone in heaven without the demands of the Gospel. There is no need to repent because God loves you just like you are! It is the cross of death to self that the Lord calls us to carry (Mark 2:17; Luke 14:27; 24:47; Mark 10:21; Matt. 10:38). The Cross is central to the message of the Christian faith. Some would try to get into the sheepfold of Christianity by some other way (John 10:1). There is no conversion without the power of the Cross. Without repentance (a turning from sin) and faith, there is no salvation, no conversion. The seed was placed on rocky soil with no salvation experience (Matt. 13:4; Isa. 53:11; Phil. 2:1-11). I believe in world missions because of the Cross (I Thess. 1:5; I Cor. 9:16; Rom. 1:16).

> ... and through Him to reconcile all things to Himself, having made peace through the blood of His cross; through Him, I say, whether things on earth or things in heaven. (Col. 1:20, NASB)

> For the message of the cross is foolishness to those who are perishing, but to us who are being saved it is the power of God. (I Cor. 1:18, NIV)

The Cross satisfies God's own demands of love and holiness! He demonstrated His love to the world by sending His Son into the world to die and give His life a ransom for the lost. He also demonstrated His hatred toward sin by the death of His Son on the Cross—a sacrifice for the sins of the world. No one could satisfy the demands of God except God Himself!

## SOME CONCLUSIONS

Holiness and love cannot be separated. God's love for the world was satisfied with the death of His Son on the Cross. His holiness and His hatred toward sin also were demonstrated on the Cross. His just wrath was an expression of His holy love. No one could satisfy the demands of God except God Himself. **He became cursed for us** (Gal. 3:13; Deut. 21:23). He rejoices that His Son did not die in vain and was approved by God Himself (Isa.53:11; Phil. 2:9-11).

### Results of the Cross

- Redemption – takes away sin – Eph. 1:7; I John 3:5
- Reconciliation – Col. 1:20
- Removes fear of death – Heb. 2:14
- Destroys works of the devil – I John 3:8; Heb. 2:14,15; Col. 2:13-15
- Gives us a hope of the Resurrection – Titus 2:13; Phil. 3:20; I Tim. 1:1
- John 14:6; 17:24
- Shows the love of God – I John 4:9

- Provides justification (right standing with God) – Rom. 5:9
- Provides healing – Matt. 8:17; Ex. 12; Psa. 105:37; Isa. 53:4
- Gives boldness – Heb. 10:19
- Gives victory – Rev. 12:10 (Sin – Rom. 6)
- Sanctified by the blood – Heb. 13:12
- Shows the love of God – I John 4:9
- Forgiveness – Matt. 18:21-35
- Hope of the Resurrection – Titus 2:3; Phil. 3:20; I Tim. 1:1; John 14:6; 17:24 (to behold My glory)
- Demands disciples to carry – Mark 8:34-38

---

Therefore: To be silent is to make the
Cross powerless!

---

Jesus was a model of what He taught!
1. The Father's **words** – John 17:8,14; 12:47; 14:10. "I speak not of myself, but the Father Who dwells in me" (John 5:30).
2. The Father's **works** – John 5:19,36. "... greater witness than John ... the Son can do nothing of Himself" (John 10:25, 32).
3. The Father's **love** (His heart) – John 17:26. "He has declared Him" (John 1:18). "... to know Me, is to know My Father" (John 14:7-10; 8:19).
4. The Father's **glory** – John 17:22. "Honor you have given Me, I give to them ..."
5. Prays for them – John 17:9,15
6. Sends them into the world as He was sent – John 17:18
7. He Sanctifies Self so that the disciples would be sanctified – John 17:19
8. He is One (Unity) with His Father – John 17:21 (He did the will of the Father; "*I and My Father are One,*" John 4:23; 10:30.)

The message and the ministry of Christ was the Kingdom of God, which included healing, casting out devils, and raising the dead (Matt. 9:35)! The Church is the Body of Christ, the fullness of Christ (I Cor. 12:12-17; Eph. 4:4-12; Col. 1:18-42 ... ***Christ in you****, v. 27*). We are His ambassadors (II Cor. 5:20). We are to glorify Christ in His word and works. We are on His mission, not our own. We represent Him on the earth—either good or bad.[6]

---

[6] Eph. 1:22,23

We are the fullness of Christ here on earth. He has no one else to represent Him except you and me, His Church. We are here to fully express Christ on earth for His glory alone…in our life, gifts, words…to glorify Christ. The world can only see Christ through His Church. He has given us His mandate to **preach, heal the sick, cleanse the lepers, cast out demons,** and even **raise the dead** (Matt. 10:8). We are His heart that feels, His hands that do, His feet that go, His mouth that speaks, His body that identifies with mankind. We are the incarnation of Christ when we pray in His Name, pleading His cause for others. When we go around the world or to our next door neighbor to preach the Gospel, or share the love of God and witness of Christ on our jobs or school, whether we preach to crowds or to one (as Jesus did so many times), even when we are silent, but speak volumes with our life … it is Christ *IN* you! He is the Model. We follow in His steps. We are the incarnation of Christ—Christ here on earth today! What the world sees in Christ is His Church, faltering and yet triumphant!

We are to model Christ. How do we make the application? How do we represent Christ, the Model Missionary, as He represented His Father in His life, words, deeds, and ministry? We are the Body of Christ to glorify Him in all things … **the fullness of Him that fills all in all** (Col. 1:18; Eph. 1:23). We are to represent Him as His ambassadors, representing Him to the world in word and deed (II Cor. 5:20). **Do all for the glory of God** (I Cor. 10:31). We are to make Christ present in our world (Mark 16:17-20; John 14:12; Acts 5:12).

# CHAPTER THREE

# Anointed by the Spirit[7]

All that Jesus did, He did because He was anointed by the Spirit. Jesus was supernaturally born of the Spirit. He was **conceived** of the Holy Spirit in the womb of Mary (Luke 1:13,35) as a fulfillment of prophecy (Ex. 40:34; Isa. 7:4). He was the eternal Word become flesh, a body prepared by God (Heb. 10:5).

In Matthew 3:16, when Jesus was baptized in water, *the Spirit descended on Him like a dove.* He was **anointed** by the Spirit while being baptized by John the Baptist and praying, *never to depart* (Luke 3:21, 22). He was anointed by the Holy Spirit before He began His public ministry. No miracles were done before the anointing! It was prophesied that He would be anointed by the Spirit (Isa. 61:1-3). These were two separate experiences. He was born of the Spirit. He was anointed by the Spirit for ministry. As the Anointed One, He was led *(driven)* by the Spirit to the desert (Luke 4:1) to be tempted by Satan, and He returned in the power of the Spirit to begin His ministry (Luke 4:14).

It was by the power of the Holy Spirit that Jesus cast out devils (Luke 11:29; Matthew 12:28 *...cast out demons by the Spirit of God...*). Everything He did was in the power of the Holy Spirit, not in Himself. He was leaving us a model to be dependent upon the Holy Spirit in our lives and ministry. Again, Jesus began His public ministry only after the anointing of the Holy Spirit. He was *strengthened by the Spirit* (Heb. 9:4), *led by the Spirit* (Luke 4:1; Matt 4:1 – even *into the wilderness*), and filled with the *joy* of the Spirit to overflowing (Luke 10:21). The Spirit was given to Him without measure.

He ministered through the gifts of the Holy Spirit: *<u>Discerning of spirits</u>* (Matt. 16:22,23); the *<u>Word of Knowledge</u>* (John 1:47; 4:171 18; Mark 5:30); the *<u>Word of Wisdom</u>* (John 8:4-7; Luke 5:4-10 – a carpenter tells a fisherman where to fish; Luke 20:20-26); *<u>Faith</u>* (Matt. 17:21;

---

[7] John 3:34; Luke 2:32; Mark 1:10; Acts 1:8; 10:38

**4:31)**; ***Prophecy, Healings, and Miracles*** (evident in the ministry of Jesus; **Matt.16:22,23**). His ***preaching and teaching were through the Holy Spirit*** (**Acts 1:2**). He taught and gave commandments by the Holy Spirit. *It is the Spirit who gives life; the flesh profits nothing. The words that I speak to you are spirit, and they are life* (**John 16:33**). This is why people said, *No man ever spoke like this man* (John 7:46).

> *For since He Whom God has sent speaks the words of God [proclaims God's own message], God does not give Him His Spirit sparingly or by measure, but boundless is the gift God makes of His Spirit! (Deut. 18:18; John 3:34, AMP).*

He ministered because God was with Him, not because He was God! But, although He was God, He chose to minister as a man in total dependence upon the Holy Spirit! What a lesson for each of us (Luke 4:18,19)!

---

> "Jesus Christ obtained power for His divine works not by His inherent deity, but by His anointing through the Holy Spirit. He was subject to the same conditions as other men."
> —R. A. Torrey, *What the Bible Teaches*

---

We should not ever get them confused. There are denominations that exist because they do not believe this truth—that there is a distinction or difference with the **Breath** for life (***born again***) and the **Baptism** in the Holy Spirit with the speaking in other tongues recorded in Acts 2:4. Jesus commanded the disciples to wait for the Gift His Father promised (Acts 1:4, 8). The disciples had already received the gift of the Spirit for salvation. Jesus breathed into them in the Upper Room and said, *Receive ye the Holy Spirit.* This was an **Impartation of Life** recorded in John 20. Pentecost baptism was a second gift. It was an **Impartation of Power**.

The disciples had experienced the Holy Spirit's indwelling presence when Jesus *breathed* on them and said, *receive the Holy Spirit* (John 20:21). The verb tense is an *aorist tense*. It speaks of an immediate experience: they were born again! Pentecost was to come later. (Luke 24:49; Mark 16:15-20; Acts 1:8) Spiritual life came to them just as Adam experienced life when God *breathed* into him the breath of life *and man became a living soul* (Gen. 2:7). Also, they fail to see that Jesus is our Example: He was born of the Spirit (Luke 1:35) and later, at the age of 30, He was anointed by the Spirit.

It was a fulfillment of the promise of Christ to the disciples, *for He (the Holy Spirit) is with you and shall be in you (John 14:17)*. The Promise was fulfilled. (Acts 1:14)

Paul, speaking to the Ephesian church, asked if they had received the Holy Spirit *since* they believed. Paul noticed something lacking. Apollos, the teacher at Ephesus, was *a learned man*. He was *mighty in the Scriptures*. He was *instructed in the way of the Lord and burning with spiritual zeal, he spoke and taught diligently and accurately the things concerning Jesus, though he was acquainted only with the baptism of John* (Acts 18:24,25, AMP). He was an accomplished scholar with enthusiasm *(boiling over in spirit)*. He was fervent and accurate, faithful and accomplished. Yet he lacked power in his preaching. John's religion was a cold-water gospel of baptism in water only. Something was lacking. They had the Christian piety, their religion was marked by strict integrity and severe morality, penitence, and godly fear, and faithfulness in service—but all without the power of the Holy Spirit, all without Pentecost! They lived by rule, not by greater illumination and demonstration of the Spirit. Religion was a joyless burden. Skilled without **Pentecost**. Trained with **no Pentecost**.

## ILLUSTRATIONS

The Samaritans were saved under the ministry of Philip (Acts 8:5-8,12). They were baptized with the Holy Spirit under the ministry of Peter and John some days later (Acts 8:14-17). **Paul** was converted on the road to Damascus by a personal vision of the resurrected Christ (Acts 9:3-9). He was baptized in the Holy Spirit under the ministry of Ananias three days later (Acts 9:17-19).

> *But when the Father sends the Counselor as my representative — and by the Counselor I mean the Holy Spirit — he will teach you everything and will remind you of everything I myself have told you. (John 14:26, NLT)*

The blessing of Pentecost is the blessing of fullness. It is the blessing of joy. It changes us from being somewhat frightened as the disciples were in the Upper Room to being bold and courageous. Ask Peter, James, and John. They were deeply attached to Jesus Christ before Pentecost. They had left all for Christ's sake, and were still without Pentecost. They believed on the Lord Jesus Christ, were witnesses of His death and His resurrection, but without Pentecost. They were workers—stewards, preachers, evangelists, workers of miracles—all without the Pentecostal experience. There are many today who are experiencing the same. Then they heard the Promise of the Spirit and set themselves to claim by faith, to wait and pray according to the Promise given by Christ, until they experienced Pentecost. They were filled with the Holy Spirit.

There are those in the ministry today who are being used powerfully by God in ministry without the Pentecostal experience of Acts 2:4. They have an intense love for the Lord and are faithful in ministry. We are members of the same Body, and love the same Lord.

**The Holy Spirit is the Executor of Missions**! When Jesus gave His last command on earth in Acts 1:8, to be filled with the Holy Spirit, He was saying that to fulfill His mission on earth, the Church needs to experience Pentecost. **There is no mission without the Holy Spirit**, not only at Pentecost but today. The disciples had already preached, healed, and cast out devils while Jesus was on earth. Now they and we need the Holy Spirit to empower us as Jesus did while He was on earth. **It was the anointing, the Holy Spirit, that gave Jesus the power to witness and to do the work of His Father**. It is the same anointing that we need to fulfill His love and mission to the world. He was given in the place of Jesus. When they experienced the Baptism in the Holy Spirit, there was a spontaneous overflow of missions—*they went everywhere preaching the Gospel...* (Acts 2:1-4).

The anointing with oil is found throughout the Old Testament. The prophets were anointed with oil (I Kings 19:16). Priests were always anointed with oil (Ex. 30:30; 40:13-15; Lev. 8:122,30; 16:32) and kings were often anointed (I Sam. 10:1; 16:3,13; II Sam. 5:3; I Kings 1:34; 10:15; II Kings 9:3). The special oil was a symbol of the Holy Spirit used for the anointing. It speaks of the anointing of the Holy Spirit today (I John 2:20).

> *And the remnant of the oil that is in the priest's hand he shall pour upon the head of him that is to be cleansed: and the priest shall make atonement for him before the Lord. (Lev. 14:18)*

In the Old Testament, the Holy Spirit's coming was prophesied. Peter mentions the prophecy of Joel 2:28,29 to answer questions at the Day of Pentecost about the Baptism in the Holy Spirit. What happened was new, but it had been prophesied that there would be a fullness of the Spirit given to the people of God.

> *And it shall come to pass afterward that I will pour out My Spirit on all flesh; Your sons and your daughters shall prophesy, your old men shall dream dreams, your young men shall see visions. And also on*

*My menservants and on My maidservants will pour out My Spirit in those days. (Joel 2:28,29)*

Before the disciples were told to go to the whole world and make disciples, they were told to wait in the city of Jerusalem, to wait for the promise of the enabling power of the Holy Spirit as Jesus was anointed before public ministry (Luke 24:49; Acts 2:4). What was the driving force of the New Testament Church? It was not the command, but the power of the Holy Spirit.

On the Day of Pentecost, He gave power and unity to the Church, a reversal of Babel, which had brought confusion. God has provided for us the same anointing that He gave Jesus. Only His was without limit (John 3:34; Heb. 1:8)! It is the same anointing that we need to fulfill His love and mission to make Christ present in our world. Pentecost brought a spontaneous overflow of missions (Acts 8:4 ...***they went everywhere preaching the Gospel***). The power of the Spirit was ever present in the Book of Acts. This is seen in Samaria (Acts 8), in the Cornelius account (Acts 10, recounted in chapter 11), and in Ephesus (Acts 19). In Acts 8 and 19 this impartation came with the laying on of hands. In Acts 10, it came spontaneously while the Gospel was being preached. In Acts 8 and 19, the Spirit came upon the recipients subsequent to salvation. Before he was filled with the Spirit, Peter cowered in the presence of a little maiden who said, "You're a disciple." Peter was afraid, intimidated, and He denied Jesus three times before the rooster crowed. But after Peter was baptized in the Holy Spirit, He stood up before the crowd and said, "*You killed Him. You crucified Him,* ***but God has raised Him up, and there is no other name under heaven given among men by which we must be saved***" (Acts 4:8-12).

The Early Church crossed religious boundaries by the direction of the Holy Spirit. Philip heard the voice of the Spirit in Acts 8:29: ***The Spirit said go near....*** In Acts 10:19, ***The Spirit said ...*** to Peter to go to the household of Cornelius. He again reaffirms it to the church in Jerusalem, defending his going by saying, ...***the Spirit told me to go and not to worry....*** Paul and Barnabas on a missionary journey were ***forbidden of the Holy Spirit*** on two occasions. It was because the Spirit had them go to Macedonia instead of going to Asia. It was the Holy Spirit who guided the Early Church with resolving tensions. They chose men ***full of wisdom and the Holy Spirit*** to be deacons and leave the apostles free for prayer and the Word (Acts 6:4). The Spirit of the Lord spoke to the Church for missionary work. ***As they were worshiping the Lord and fasting that the Spirit said, separate now for Me Barnabas and Saul for the work to which I have called them*** (Acts 13:2, AMP).

As the Son is our Advocate with the Father (I John 2:1), so the Holy Spirit is the Advocate of the Son here on earth representing Christ on earth (John 14:16,26). He pleads His cause, defends His Name, and guards His interests of His Kingdom on earth. He personally represents Christ on earth, constantly on our side to strengthen and help us make Christ present in our world. The Holy Spirit executes God's plan of redemption. We obey. The Holy Spirit executes and pleads our cause before God (John 15:26; 16:7). He glorifies Christ (John 16:14,15).

The Holy Spirit is the Executor of God's plan of redemption (John 15:26; 16:7). We obey. He glorifies Christ (John 16:14,15). He makes Christ present in our world. On the Day of Pentecost, seventeen nations heard the Sound. The Holy Spirit guided the Early Church by resolving tensions, guided the Early Church to specific fields, and forbade them from going to other fields. (Acts 16:6,7) He was and is the Administrator of missions, the supreme Strategist, sending laborers and directing the harvesting (Acts 13:1-3; I Cor. 3:9). He gave supernatural power to preach, to experience miracles, and to live a Christ-like lifestyle. He is the One who initiated the missionary work as the Lord's Executor here on earth (I Cor. 12:4; Acts 20:28; 15:28; 14:27). The Early Church had power and boldness, even with persecution and martyrdom (Acts 1:8).

Jesus chose not to minister on earth as God but as a man through the anointing of the Holy Spirit. Because Jesus ministered as a man full of the Holy Spirit, we also can be filled with the Holy Spirit and do the things that He did.

Peter went everywhere **preaching the Gospel with the Holy Spirit sent from above** ...(I Pet. 1:13). Paul said that **the Gospel came to you in power and in the Holy Spirit** (I Thess. 1:5,6) and the ministry came to the Corinthian church ... **by the Holy Spirit and sincere love** (II Cor. 6:6). Again we see the Holy Spirit predominant with the Church, **God also bearing them witness with signs and wonders, and with divers miracles, and gifts of the Holy Spirit** (Heb. 2:4). **He shall testify of Me** (John 15:26). The Holy Spirit was prophesied in Isaiah 44:3—**I will pour water upon him that is thirsty.... And in** Joel 2:28,29—**I will pour out of My Spirit upon all flesh**.... In the first teaching of Jesus in Matt. 5:6, He said that **those who hunger and thirst shall be filled**. In the last book of the Bible, an invitation is given by God Himself: ...**if you are thirsty, come** (Rev. 22:17)! John says that **you have an anointing** (I John 2:20, 27), and we have been **anointed, sealed, and have been given the Holy Spirit in our hearts as a security deposit and guarantee of the fulfillment of the promise** (II Cor. 1:21,22, AMP).

Paul, in preaching the Gospel, answered both the Jews who demanded a sign and the Greeks who sought after wisdom. When Paul preached, He satisfied both groups by preaching the Gospel.

> *For Jews request a sign, and Greeks seek after wisdom; but we preach Christ crucified, to the Jews a stumbling block and to the Greeks foolishness, but to those who are called, both Jews and Greeks, Christ the power of God and the wisdom of God. Because the foolishness of God is wiser than men, and the weakness of God is stronger than men. (I Cor. 1:22-25)*

The Holy Spirit inspires and enables all efforts to fulfill Christ's commission to disciple the nations. This was to be the means to fulfill Christ's commission until His return. (Acts 1:8)

At Pentecost, the Spirit of power (***dunamis***) was given to them to bear witness unto Christ. The growth of the Early Church came through the power and work of the Holy Spirit. For examples: Philip (Acts 8:26-29); Peter (Acts 10); missionary outreach from Antioch (Acts 13:1-6) and Europe (Acts 16:6-10,16,17); Ephesus (Acts 19:1-6); crossing geographical and cultural barriers (Acts 2:47; 5:13; 6:7; 9:31); Paul and Barnabas (Acts 15:12). All this was prophesied (Joel 2:28-32; Acts 2:17-21; John 14:12,16; 16:7,8).

The Spirit inspires worship (Phil. 3:3) and was even needed for ***serving tables*** (Acts 6:1-6). The book of Acts also records miracles through the power of the Holy Spirit—Ananias and Sapphira fall down dead (5:1-10), Peter pronounced a curse on Simon Magus in Samaria (8:20-23), Paul cursed Elymas in Cyprus (13:10-12) with devastating results. It was through the power of the Holy Spirit that the sick were healed (Acts 3:1-10). He inspired the preaching of the Word (Acts 4:31) and gifted the Church for ministry and its leadership (Rom. 12:23-29; I Cor. 12:1-3; 14; Ephesians 4:11,12). The Spirit changes lives: ... ***into the same image (of Christ) from glory to glory*** (II Cor. 3:17, 18). He ***bears witness*** (Rom. 8:16,17). He produces the life of Christ in the ***fruit of the Spirit*** (Gal. 5:22,23). He gives the words to speak (Matt. 10:19,20; Acts 6:10; 7:51-57, Stephen; Acts 5:9, Peter). He directed the early Apostles to their perspective field of ministry from the general plan (Acts 1:8) and to the respective plan (Acts 16:6-10; 22:18; 18:9-11; 15:7, Peter to the Gentiles).

Today, missionaries can hear the Spirit's nudging or a clear voice to follow Christ in obedience to the Great Commission to go to mega-cities, or to small unknown villages, or even caves, to many or few, to preach the

Gospel in crusades or to translate the Scriptures to an obscure language group—all directed by the Holy Spirit. In the Book of Acts, the Holy Spirit is mentioned fifty-five times!

When we are on His mission to the world; the Holy Spirit goes before us. He is the Helper and Strengthener. He is the ***Paracletos,*** meaning someone called in for help to render a service (John 14:16,26; 15:26; 16:7). He is the Counsel for Defense of an accused person. He is our Advocate, the supernatural Defense Attorney. Jesus is our Advocate with the Father (I John 2:1) and the Spirit is the One who intercedes for the Son here on earth (Rom. 8:26,27). He represents Christ when convicting the sinner of sin, righteousness, and of judgment (John 16:7-11). He is the One who calls the lost to salvation through the preaching of the Gospel.

It is interesting to note that the **Great Commission** is not mentioned in the Acts of the Apostles, not because it was unimportant, but because it was un-necessary to mention it. The Church did not need an external command. They were fulfilling the command of Christ in the power of the Holy Spirit (Acts 2:4; 5:28)!

The New Testament has as much to say about the power of the Gospel as it does about the truth of the Gospel. The ministry of Jesus brought together the declaration of truth and the demonstration of power. He forgave the man sick of the palsy (Mark 2:5) and healed him of his sickness (Mark 2:10,11). Jesus was anointed with ***the Holy Spirit and power*** (Acts 10:38). Paul says that He was ***declared to be the Son of God with power according to the spirit of holiness, by the resurrection of the dead*** (Rom. 1:4). Jesus possesses all power in heaven and in earth—to forgive sins (Mark 2:10), to impart eternal life (John 17:2), and to execute judgment (John 5:22,27).

The resources of the Church are in ***the supply of the Spirit*** (Phil. 1:19). It is in Him who makes ***greater works*** possible than those of Christ while here on earth. He is the Spirit of God, the Spirit of Truth, the Spirit of Witness, of Conviction, of Power, of Holiness, of Life, of Wisdom, of Revelation, of Promise, of Adoption, of Grace, of Glory, of Prophecy. It is not in man-made, man-centered, man-powered missions. It is only in the ***fullness of the Spirit*** that we can experience the abundance of God's provision to fulfill the mission of Christ here on earth. The gifts and ministries in the Church are given by the Holy Spirit (Eph. 4:1-13; I Cor. 12-14). Peter ***preached the Gospel with the Holy Spirit sent from above*** (I Pet. 1:12; II Cor. 6:6; I Thess. 1:5,6; Heb. 2:4). ***He shall testify of Me*** (John 15:26). The growth of the Church was not in theology only, in proclamation of truth only, but in the demonstration of power.

Here is a list of some in the Scriptures that God used for those who were anointed with Holy Spirit.

- John the Baptist – filled with the Holy Spirit from the womb (Luke 1:15)
- Mary – the Holy Spirit shall come upon you (Luke 1:35)
- Elizabeth – filled with the Holy Spirit (Luke 1:41)
- Zachariah – filled with the Holy Spirit and prophesied (Luke 1:67-79)
- Ministry of believers to look like ministry of Lord – (John 14:12)
- Church leadership – chose men full of the Holy Spirit (Acts 6:3)
- Peter — proclamation (Acts 4:8-10)
- Philip — crossing social/cultural barriers (Acts 8:26-29)
- Paul & Barnabas – the Spirit did not permit them (Acts 16)
- Missionaries – the Spirit said separate me Paul and Barnabas (Acts 13:2-4)
- Gifts of men to the Church – (Eph. 4:11-13)

**Growth of Church**: The Work of the Holy Spirit:

- Wait for the Promise – (Acts 1:8)
- Philip –to Samaria (Acts 8:26-38)
- Peter (household of Cornelius) – (Acts 10)
- Antioch – first missionary journey (Acts 13:1-6)
- Europe – Paul & Silas (Acts 15:22)
- Paul and Barnabas forbidden by the Holy Spirit (Acts 16:6-10,16,17)
- Crossed geographical and cultural barriers (Acts 2:47 cf. Acts 5:14; 6:7; 9:31)
- Ministry and gifts of the Spirit – (Romans 12:5-9; I Cor. 12-14)
- House to House – (Acts 2:46; 20:20)

> "Jesus Christ obtained power for His divine works not by His inherent deity, but by His anointing through the Holy Spirit. He was subject to the same conditions as other men."
> —R. A. Torrey, *What the Bible Teaches*

> "Jesus received the Spirit in fullness, with nothing held back, and He alone has universal authority. However, since this enduement of the Holy Spirit is given to Him whom God has sent, John 20:21 would suggest a similar unlimited resource of Holy Spirit fullness is available to obedient disciples of Jesus."
> —Jack Hayford

Because Jesus ministered as a man full of the Holy Spirit we also can be filled with the Holy Spirit and do the things that He did. Jesus Christ obtained power for His divine works not because He was God incarnate, but by His anointing through the power of the Holy Spirit. He was subject to the same conditions as other men.

How am I to receive what those in the early century called "**The Blessing**." You have been born again as the disciples were. Jesus gave the command to wait until they were endued with power. How can I receive the fullness of the Spirit?

**First**: **Salvation** is of grace through **faith**. We are justified by faith. Now, do we believe the Promise of Pentecost is for me today, if I have not received it yet? Do you believe that Christ is able and willing to give you His Promise of Pentecost? Faith is an attitude of mind and heart, as well as an act of obedience to what is believed to be the truth. Faith is personally grasping what is truth and responding to it. Faith says, "Yes," to the Promise, even though I have not yet experienced it. The disciples believed the Promise. They waited *UNTIL* they received the Promise because they believed the Word of Christ. They did not know it would be ten days. It could have been one day or one month. Faith said, "Yes," to the Person Who made the Promise—Jesus Christ Himself ... and He does not lie! Do I believe the Promise of Pentecost is for today ... for me?

**Second**: **Repentance** Peter says in his first message after Pentecost, "Repent, and let every one of you be baptized in the name of Jesus Christ for the remission of sins; and you shall receive the gift of the Holy Spirit" (Acts 2:38). When one begins to wait upon the Lord, it may begin with the conviction of sin ... maybe not an obvious transgression of the Law or sins of the flesh, but also sins of the spirit, things that are in disobedience to the will of God, things not surrendered—selfishness. They must all be surrendered to the supreme authority of Christ. Repent and ask Christ's forgiveness. Without Him being exalted, crowned, and glorified, there can be no Pentecost. I can only imagine what went on for the ten days in the Upper Room. James and John may have had to ask forgiveness for wanting a right and left hand in the Kingdom of God above the other disciples. Peter had to ask forgiveness for his denial of the Lord. The Bible says that before Pentecost, they were in one accord and in one place.

**Third:** We need to ***Ask in Faith***. In Luke 11, Jesus gives a parable on prayer. A friend arrives late at night to request bread at midnight. He keeps pounding and will not stop until the door is opened and he receives his need. Luke 11:13 (NASB) says, *"If you then, being evil, know how to give good* *gifts to your children, how much more will your heavenly Father give the Holy Spirit to those who ask Him?"* Believe Christ that His Promise of Pentecost is for you. James 4:4 says that *you have not because you ask not.... Wait upon the Lord.* Jesus says that we are to ask, believing that whatever the circumstances, when He gives the Promise of Pentecost, He will fulfill it with His Presence. Again, the disciples keep pounding the door of heaven for 10 days until they received the fullness of the Spirit in fulfillment of the Promise. It is in that context that He says *that He will give the Holy Spirit to them that ask of Him* (Luke 11:13).

**Fourth**: There is **Thirst** ... a hungering after God and what He has for us brings us to the point of waiting. Are we satisfied with our experience, or do we desire more? Do we desire wells of water springing up?

> *"If anyone thirsts, let him come to Me and drink. He who believes in Me, as the Scripture has said, out of his heart will flow rivers of living water." But this He spoke concerning the Spirit, whom those believing in Him would receive; for the Holy Spirit was not yet given, because Jesus was not yet glorified. (John 7:37-39)*

**Fifth**: We are to **Receive by Faith**. We wait until we receive, because we believe the Promise. Those in the Upper Room believed the first day they began waiting upon the Lord. They did not stop after one day, two days, three days ... etc. They believed the Promise and received it by faith until they experienced the fullness of the Spirit. Faith claims and takes.

> *And whatever you ask for in prayer, having faith and [really] believing, you will receive. (Matt 21:22, AMP)*

> *Through Christ Jesus, God has blessed the Gentiles with the same blessing he promised to Abraham, so that we who are believers might receive the promised Holy Spirit through faith. (Gal 3:14, AMP)*

> *(When he said "living water," he was speaking of the Spirit, who would be given to everyone believing in him. But the Spirit had not yet been given, because Jesus had not yet entered into his glory. (John 7:39, AMP)*

**Sixth: Continuous Obedience.**

> *And we are His witnesses to these things, and so also is the Holy Spirit whom God has given to those who obey Him. (Acts 5:32, NKJV)*

> ... but be continually filled with fresh oil of the Holy Spirit.... (Eph. 5:18)

> Everyone who is thirsty, come to the waters and he who has no money come, buy and eat. Yes, come buy priceless spiritual wine and milk without money and without price (simply for the self-surrender that accepts the blessing). (Isa. 55:1; cf. Rev. 21:6,7; 22:17)

The blessing of Pentecost can be lost when we fail to have continuous obedience. The Spirit continues to flow through us when we are continually hearing and obeying His voice. To be Spirit-filled is to be Spirit-ruled. What a joy to be ruled by the Spirit ... under His authority and power. The Ephesian church is an example (Acts 19:1-6).

> After this prayer, the meeting place shook, and they were all filled with the Holy Spirit. Then they preached the word of God with boldness. (Acts 4:31, NLT)

**Question**: Have you been filled with the Holy Spirit since you believed? If not, do you desire to be filled with the Spirit? Do you believe the Promise made by Christ Himself that He will baptize you with the Holy Spirit? If you have been baptized in the Holy Spirit, the Spirit speaks to us to be continually filled with the Spirit. It is easy to become professional in our witness, our preaching, our praying, our service to the Lord ... without power or without zeal ... something we do mechanically, rather than with the Spirit's aid. Is there a deeper hunger for more of the Spirit in our lives in our passion of love to Christ? More love for souls, a greater manifestation of God's power in your life and in the ministry, more love for one another, more of a unity of the Spirit in our homes and in the church, greater release of the gifts of the Spirit ... more of God?

> Don't be drunk with wine, because that will ruin your life. Instead, let the Holy Spirit fill and control you (continually). (Eph. 5:18, NLT)

## WHAT ARE THE RESULTS AND THE EVIDENCE OF GOD'S PROMISE?[8]

The power of the Holy Spirit was not to glorify and make the preacher famous, but to glorify Christ as Savior and Lord. The Holy Spirit is the manifested power and the glory of God. He is also called the "Anointing."

---

[8] Joel 2:27,28; Luke 24:49; Acts 1:8; 2:1-4; 4:33

## 1) INITIAL EVIDENCE

Jesus promised they would receive power after the power of the Holy Spirit would come upon them. Speaking with other tongues was the immediate evidence of the supernatural experience of the Baptism with the Holy Spirit. On the day of Pentecost, there were several nations represented who heard the Gospel in their own language magnifying the works of God. They were astounded and perplexed and surprised in what they experienced. They understood the meaning of the words, but not the purpose. Others mocked. All of this was the fulfillment of the prophecy given in Joel 2:28-33. On three occasions, it is specifically recorded that the believers spoke with other tongues when the Holy Spirit came upon them (Acts 2:4; 10:46; 19:6). Tongues are not mentioned when the Holy Spirit came upon them, but something happened *(as yet He was fallen upon none of them: only they were baptized in the name of the Lord Jesus ... and they received the Holy Spirit)* that was noticeable (Acts 8:16-18). It was also recorded that the place was shaken under the power of the Holy Spirit (Acts 4:31). Speaking in tongues is a sign to the unbeliever (I Cor. 14:22).

## 2) A PASSION FOR SOULS AND THE POWER TO WITNESS

Before Pentecost, 120 disciples were huddled in a room. They had been disappointed but now after seeing Christ after His resurrection, they waited His promise of the power of the Holy Spirit to be a witness (**"martyr"** is the meaning of the word in the original Greek). Wherever the Church went, they had a message of salvation of Christ to win souls whether to the religious Jews, Samaritans, on the streets, or in the temple. They followed the pattern of Jesus. He came to seek and to save the lost. That was His mission and it was the mission of the Early Church to win souls to Jesus Christ as Lord.

After Pentecost, they went *everywhere preaching the Word* (Acts 1:8; 87:4; 11:18). Because of the persecution, the church scattered through the regions of Judea and Samira, except the apostles (Acts 8:1). The power changed Peter from a coward to be a fearless preacher who witnessed 3,000 and 5,000 come to Christ (Acts 2:41; 4:4). It was the power of the Holy Spirit in the preaching of the Gospel (Acts 2:14-41; 4:19,20; 5:29-33; 6:8-10; 11:22-24; 26:28,29). The first missionaries to be sent out by the church in Antioch were sent out by the Holy Spirit (Acts 13:1-4).

> *For our gospel did not come to you in word only, but also in power, and in the Holy Spirit and in much assurance ... (I Thess. 1:5)*

*And my speech and my preaching were not with persuasive words of human wisdom, but in demonstration of the Spirit and of power, that your faith should not be in the wisdom of men but in the power of God. (I Cor. 2:4,5)*

See John 15:26; 16:7; I Corinthians 2:4,5; Acts 4:31,33; I Cor. 4:20; I Thess. 1:5; John 14:16,26; Luke 24:49; Matt. 3:11

*And they went out and preached everywhere, the Lord working with them and confirming the word through the accompanying signs. Amen. (Mark 16:20, NLT)*

*We cannot stop telling about everything we have seen and heard." The council then threatened them further.... For everyone was praising God for this miraculous sign—the healing of a man who had been lame for more than forty years. (Acts 4:20-22, NLT)*

## 3) PRAYER

After Pentecost, there was an emphasis on prayer. It followed the pattern of Jesus who was a man of prayer (Acts 3:1; 4:23-31; 6:4; 10:9; Rom. 8:26; Jude 20; Eph. 6:18; I Cor. 14:1-17).

## 4) MIRACLES

Jesus performed many miracles, yet He said that **greater than these shall ye do because I go to My Father** (John 14:12). The ministry of signs and wonders did not cease with the ministry of Christ and the apostles. They continued after His resurrection. Miracles continued to be manifested throughout the book of Acts (Acts 6:8 – Stephen; Acts 3:6; 4:22 – Peter and John; 9:33-35 – Peter). God continues to bear witness **with signs and wonders, with various miracles, and gifts of the Holy Spirit** (Heb. 2:4).

It was the power of the Spirit that He would give the power to be a martyr and also to preach, to heal, to cast out devils, and even raise the dead (Luke 10:20). There have been several verified instances of people being raised from the dead (Reinhard Bonnke). Harry Gomes from India has verified five people resurrected from the dead with 11% Christians in India (Joel News International, 8/15/07). The Bible says that we have an anointing (II Cor. 1:21; I John 2:20). The Bible also says that we need to be continually filled with the Holy Spirit. If we had a wonderful Baptism, as I had as a child, I need to be continually filled with the Spirit, continually walking in humility and dependency, and hungering and thirsting after God—being filled continually with Him!

## 4) SPIRITUAL GIFTS

The Holy Spirit also gives gifts to the believer. They are to be accompanied by the fruit of the Spirit of love (I Cor. 13:1-3). The gifts of the Holy Spirit mentioned in I Cor. 12:8-10 are:

- Word of Wisdom
- Word of Knowledge
- Faith
- Healings
- Working of Miracles
- Prophecy
- Discerning of Spirits
- Tongues
- Interpretation of Tongues

No gift is unimportant, as no member in the Body is unimportant and unnecessary. When God adopts us into His Family, He has given the gift of His choosing to each of us for the common good (I Cor. 12:7). Love is to be under the umbrella of love and ***the manifestation of the Spirit is given to each one for the profit of all (***I Cor. 12:7).

See also: I Corinthians 12-14; I Peter 4:10,11; Acts 19:11; Hebrews 6:4,5; Acts 5:12; 14:3; Hebrews 2:4; John 14:12; Romans 15:19; 8:15; II Cor. 3:17 (freedom of ministry).

# CHAPTER FOUR

# Prayer

**In Eternity**—World missions began in a prayer meeting before time (Psa. 2:8; 22;27; 72:8). All missions began at the Throne Room of heaven!

> *Ask of Me, and I will give you the nations for Your inheritance, and the ends of the earth for Your possession. (Psa. 2:8)*

**In Time**—See Luke 6:12; 22:31-34 (praying for Peter), 39-46; Heb. 5:7,8; John 17:18-20 (praying for the church); Isa. 53:10-12.

Jesus also came in answer to the prayers of Simeon and Anna (Luke 2:25-29). The whole nation had prayed for the Messiah. Jesus' public ministry began with 40 days of fasting and prayer in the Temptation (Luke 4:1-14). As He was being baptized by John the Baptist, as He was ***praying, the heavens was opened and the Holy Spirit descended*** (Luke 3:21)! In His life, before He preached, He prayed (Luke 3:21,22). Each of the Gospel writers shows us moments when Jesus was in prayer.

Jesus prayed to show His dependence upon His Father. ***The Son can do nothing by himself. He does only what he sees the Father doing. Whatever the Father does, the Son also does*** (John 5:19, NLT). ***He emptied Himself (Phil. 2:6,7).*** Throughout the Biblical record, we have Jesus rising before morning and ***departed to a solitary place to pray*** (Mark 1:35; Luke 5:16; 9:18,23—with Peter and John). ***He went into a mountain to pray ... continued all night in prayer to God.*** And in the morning He chose His disciples (Luke 6:12). When He had a successful ministry of healing and miracles, instead of glorying in His success, ***He withdrew Himself into the wilderness, and prayed*** (Luke 6:16). After He fed the 5,000, ***He prayed*** (Luke 9:18). After He raised Lazarus from the dead, **He prayed** (John 11:41,42). He went alone to the mountain to **pray** (Matt. 14:23; Mark 6:46). When the day was unusually busy He prayed. ***And when he had sent the multitudes away, he went up into a mountain apart to pray:***

*and when the evening was come, he was there alone* (Matt. 14:23). When in great crisis and turning points in His life, **He prayed** (Luke 9:28, 29—Transfiguration). When the people wanted to make Him king by force, He departed into the mountain *to pray* (John 6:15). He prayed more privately than publicly (John 6:15). ***Who in the days of His flesh, when He offered up prayers and supplications with strong crying and tears unto Him that was able to save Him from death, and was heard in that He feared...*** (Heb. 5:7, KJV).

He prays near the end of His life (John 17:18-20). Ten times in the book of Luke we find Him praying. He prays for Peter and His disciples (Luke 22:31, 32; 9,15; Heb. 5:7) and in Mark 6:46 ... ***departed to a mountain to pray.*** He prayed with great agony; sweat became as it were drops of blood at Gethsemane (Matt. 26:36-45; Mk. 14:32-42; Luke 22:39-46). Three of His seven sayings on the cross were prayers (Luke 23:34). He made ***continual intercession for the transgressors*** (Isa. 53:10-12). He lived a life of prayer, leaving us an example. All His words and deeds, His miracles and teachings were answers to prayer and grew out of His continual and perfect inner prayer life of intimacy with His Father! ***It is mentioned 40 times in the Gospel records that Jesus prayed!*** (In Matthew 9 times, Mark 13 times, Luke 13 times, John 5 times.) Of these references, there are 23 separate occasions in Jesus' three-year ministry that He retreated to His prayer life. All His recorded prayers are short, except the High Priestly prayer of John 17.

> *I do not pray for these alone, but also for those who will believe in Me through their word. (John 17:20)*
>
> *... and was numbered with the transgressors; yet he bore the sin of many, and makes intercession for the transgressors. (Isa. 53:12, ESV)*

## In Eternity

The Holy Spirit is a praying Spirit (Rom. 8:26,27). In Zechariah 12:10, the Spirit is called ***the Spirit of grace and supplication.***

> *For He testifies: "You are a priest forever According to the order of Melchizedek. ... Therefore He is also able to save to the uttermost those who come to God through Him, since He always lives to make intercession for them. (Heb. 7:17,25)*

## APPLICATION

Jesus exhorts us to *fast* (Matt. 6:16-18) and pray *persistently* (Luke 18:1-8), in *faith* (Matt. 21:21,22), in His **Name** (John 14:14; 16:23), with *sincerity* (Matt. 13:21-33), according to *His will* (I John 5:14), and *in unity* (Matt. 18:19). We will speak of praying for missions later.

When Jesus wanted to start His worldwide mission, He called a strategy session. He called a **PRAYER MEETING**. He said, *tarry until ...* (Luke 24:49). The Early Church responded. After ten days, **these all continued with one accord and in constant prayer** (Acts 1:14). They continued until they received the Promise of the Holy Spirit (Acts 2:1-4). The poured out Spirit came as a result of their obedience in prayer, repentance, and faith. (In Joel 2, the promised poured-out Spirit is spoken of in the context of repentance.) Three thousand souls were the immediate result!

The Early Church was a missionary church. Prayer was not a ministry but its primary ministry. After the initial outpouring of the Spirit, the Church continued to make prayer the foundation of its ministry. After persecution, the Church was called to prayer (Acts 4:23-31).

Following conversions, *prayer* was always in focus and primary. *...and they continued steadfastly in the apostles' doctrine, fellowship, the breaking of bread, and in prayers* (Acts 2:42). This verse gives us elements of the Early Church in its mission to the world, i.e., *apostles' doctrine, fellowship, breaking of bread*, and *prayer*. Only one of these four elements reaches beyond the group—*prayer!* Studying *doctrine*, having *fellowship*, and the *breaking of bread* were ministries *within* the group.

The results? *And the Lord added daily to the Church such as should be saved* (Acts 2:47). When there was persecution, it led to *prayer* (Acts 4:28-31).

> *All the believers devoted themselves to the apostles' teaching, and to fellowship, and to sharing in meals (including the Lord's Supper), and to prayer. (Acts 2:42)*

> *After this prayer, the meeting place shook, and they were all filled with the Holy Spirit. Then they preached the word of God with boldness. (Acts 4:31, NLT)*

When there was division in the Church concerning the care for widows, the leadership made the **Word** and **prayer** their primary emphasis (Acts 6:2-4). It resulted in **great power** (Acts 8:10), **great grace** (Acts 4:33), and **great fear** (Acts 5:5). When the Church went through its second crisis in

Acts 6 (the first being covetousness, hypocrisy, lying, tempting and testing the Holy Spirit), the apostles designated others *to attend to serving tables and superintending the distribution of foods* (Acts 6:3, AMP). It was not that the apostles were beyond that, but they considered a higher priority for themselves. They were to *devote ourselves steadfastly to the Word and to prayer* (Acts 6:4, AMP). In Acts 8, Philip preaches, resulting in revival, while Peter and John pray that the Samaritans would receive the Holy Spirit, which they did. After Paul was converted, Ananias found him *praying*. His life and ministry were characterized by prayers and tears (Acts 20:31). ...*my heart's desire AND prayer is* ... (Rom. 9:3; 10:1).

## THE PRAYER JESUS TAUGHT HIS DISCIPLES

Jesus modeled praying for those who would believe in Him through the word of His disciples (John 17:9,10; 20,21). *As Jesus was praying in a certain place, one of His disciples said unto Him, Lord, teach us to pray, as John also taught his disciples* (Luke 11:1-4). In Luke 11 we have the disciples (we do not know which ones) asking Jesus to teach them to pray. *As Jesus was praying in a certain place, one of His disciples said unto Him, Lord, teach us to pray, as John also taught his disciples* (Luke 11:1). This is the first time the disciples ever asked to be taught anything. There is no record of them saying, "**teach us how to**" preach, teach, or cast out devils. They do not ask Christ to teach them how to pray, but *TO* pray! The disciples took notice that the key to the life and ministry of Jesus lay in His relationship with His Father and that everything Jesus did was tied directly to the throne of God (Matt. 6:9-16). Evan Roberts, a great revivalist in Wales and Scotland, had withdrawn for eight years from preaching ministry. He was asked what he was doing. He replied, *"I have been praying the prayer of the Kingdom."*

The first prayer that Jesus taught His disciples was a missions prayer.

## A. "OUR FATHER ... HALLOWED BE THY NAME" (MATT. 6:9)—WORSHIP

Just as worship is the ultimate goal of missions, praying is foundational to accomplish that goal. And prayer begins with worship! *Our Father* speaks of immanence, but *in heaven* speaks of transcendence. *To hallow* the Name of God, is to make it holy, to treat it with reverence, to adore it throughout the world, and differently from any other name, person, material, position, power, or love. It is to give it special praise and worship. By virtue of the blood of Jesus, we have entered into a new covenant. Names in the Bible often are given to people to reflect the attributes and characteristics that distinguish them. This is especially true of God. When one claims the Name of Christ as his/her own, then to honor it is to live out the character of His Name (II Tim. 2:19). It speaks of all that God is in nature and character (lips, mind, lives, families, calling, or business for His glory), for the glory of the Father (John 14:13), that our joy might be full (John 16:24). Since all is *from* Him and *through* Him, all must be *to Him* and *for Him* (Rom. 11:36).

Our Father is not ashamed to call us His own. He shows us His everlasting love and His mercies which are new every morning. We worship Him when we put our Father in a class by Himself, to cherish the Name above all other names, honor it above all other claims to our allegiance or affections, more than any other name, person, material, position, power, or love. He is the Creator and Father of us all. He has adopted us into His Family through Jesus Christ.

Missions is to see more people *hallow* (make holy) the Name, for the glory of the Father. He is the Creator and Father of us all. He has adopted us into His Family through Jesus Christ. It is for the glory of the Father *that our joy might be full* (John 14:13; John 16:24).

## B. "WHO ART IN HEAVEN" (MATT. 6:9)

We recognize the Father as sovereign with absolute authority. He holds the universe in His hands. Missions begins with knowing that our Father has ultimate authority and power over the nations.

**Note:** To *overthrow Satanic kingdom* (II Cor. 10:4). The *"high thing"* (an astrological term) is the sphere in which astrological powers are in control. Those who oppose the Gospel are held captive by demonic forces. Jesus is the Victor and Satan's kingdom shall be defeated!

> *For the weapons of our warfare are not carnal but mighty in God for pulling down strongholds, casting down arguments and every high thing that exalts itself against the knowledge of God, bringing every thought into captivity to the obedience of Christ, and being ready to punish all disobedience when your obedience is fulfilled. (II Cor. 10:4-6)*

## C. "THY KINGDOM COME" (MATT. 6:10)—REIGN OF GOD

This is a missions prayer that the **Kingdom,** the gospel of Christ, may be advanced everywhere, until the world shall be filled with His glory. It is prayer that the Kingdom of Heaven will be manifested in the hearts of men on earth. Jesus referred to it in His earthly ministry—*the **Kingdom of heaven is** near* (Matt. 3:2). This Kingdom had been prophesied that it would come (Isa. 5:16; 29:23; Ezek. 36:23; 38:23; 39:7,27; Zech. 14:8). The Kingdom advances in response to prayer, to reign; to manifest His kingly sovereignty and power as it is in heaven. It is the reign of God—His rulership in our lives, marriage, family, church, cities, nations. The Kingdom would come as a result of His Incarnation, the power and results of the Cross, the Resurrection, the power of the Holy Spirit, and His Ascension.

We pray that God would put to flight every enemy of righteousness and of His divine rule, that God alone is the King in the whole earth. We are to pray that His Kingdom of righteousness, peace, and joy in the Holy Spirit would come. It is the reign of God, His rulership in lives, marriages, families, churches, cities, a nation! God's Kingdom rules over all (Psa. 103:19), for it is an *everlasting Kingdom* (Psa. 145:13).

The word *Kingdom* here means *to reign, to rule everywhere, to be exalted above all kingdoms* (Dan. 7:14-27; Luke 9:7) *for it is an everlasting Kingdom* (Psa. 145:13). Here, in time, it begins when one is *born again* and enters into *the kingdom of God* (John 3:3,5). We are asking that God's will be done here and now in our lives!

There are only two kingdoms in the world: the *kingdom of darkness* (ruled by Satan and his emissaries) and the *Kingdom of Light* with Christ as Lord! When we pray "Thy Kingdom come," we are praying for heaven to come to earth and establish the reign of Christ. It will finally be answered when God brings human history to an end. When we pray, we also ask that God's will be done here and now, today! God's Kingdom advances in prayer that His heavenly Kingdom would rule on earth as it is in heaven. That is, that He would manifest His kingly sovereignty and power with full authority to rule universally in the hearts of mankind, in the city, and in the country! The Kingdom of Satan opposes all that God has ordained. The prayer *"Thy Kingdom come"* will also be answered when God brings human history to an end and establishes His Kingdom here on earth. His Kingdom shall prevail over all the kingdoms of this world! Hallelujah! (Rev. 11:15; Psa. 115:15,16; 24:1,2, 7-10; 47:7-9; II Tim. 2:1, 2)

**Question**: What cities and areas of your country still need God's Kingdom to come, to reign supremely and sovereignly with Jesus Christ as Lord? What unreached people groups (distinct ethnic, linguistic, social or cultural distinctions) with no church need to know Christ and the power of the Gospel? Would you pray that God's Kingdom would come to them even through you?

## Examples

*The king's heart is like a stream of water directed by the Lord; he guides it wherever he pleases. (Prov. 21:1, NLT)*

When Phillip preached a revival in Samaria, Peter and John **prayed** and the converts were baptized in the Holy Spirit (Acts 8:15). Saul was **praying** when the Lord spoke to Ananias to go and **pray** that Saul would receive his sight and be filled with the Holy Spirit (Acts 9:17). Paul's life was characterized by **prayers** and tears (Acts 20:31).

There have been changes in today's world through the prayers of God's people, e.g., in Romania, Ukraine, Russia, China, and worldwide.

The Holy Spirit is a praying Spirit (Rom. 8:26, 27, 34; Heb. 7:25; 9:24; I John 2:1). In Zechariah 12:10, the Spirit is called the **Spirit of grace and supplication**. Prayer is for the **glory of God** (John 14:13; 15:7,8) and for our **joy** (John 16:24).

## JESUS COMMANDS US TO PRAY

Prayer and evangelism are never to be separated. When Christ saw the multitude, *He was moved with compassion ... for they were as sheep without a shepherd.*

*THEREFORE, pray the Lord of the harvest that He would send forth laborers into His harvest* (Matt. 9:38; Luke 10:2,12,13; Acts 13:2). His first response: **PRAY!**

The phrase *to send them out* in verse 28 means literally *to kick them out ("ex baleo")*. The laborers are present. Pray that the Lord of the Harvest would *kick them out* to be harvesters in His field (John 17:20; Rev. 5:9)! They may be sitting in the pew, in a business, or content at home. **Pray** that the Lord would kick them out to go overseas or next door, in person or through prayer. Notice again the emphasis the Lord puts on prayer and world missions.

When God has a man or woman, who is willing to labor for Him, He will accomplish His purpose in that person and in relationship to the Kingdom of God—spiritual, not educational. God does not begin with program but with men and women.

Does the Church need laborers? **PRAY! PRAY** that God would *kick them out* as His laborers! Does the Church in your city need to reach out to every generation, to every part of society? Elderly? Students? Schools?

Communities? Pray! ***Ask and receive that your joy might be full*** (John 16:24).

We are not only to pray but to go, ***to be wise as serpents and harmless as doves,*** to expect suffering and persecution. The Holy Spirit will speak in those times of persecution. Be a bold witness and you will be rewarded generously. The Spirit of God would speak through them in times of persecution (Matt. 10:16-42). Again, what unreached people groups in your city or country need to be reached with the Gospel ***from every tribe, nation, people, nation*** (Rev. 5:9; John 17:20). Again, it begins with prayer (Acts 13:2)! In redemption, God gets the glory in worship from millions of the redeemed through the witness of His servants.

> *I do not pray for these alone, but also for those who will believe in Me through their word. (John 17:20)*

## **FASTING**

Jesus modeled fasting when He began His ministry with fasting for 40 days in the wilderness. The disciple is not above his Lord (Luke 6:40). There are different fasts mentioned in the Bible (Moses, Jehoshaphat, Daniel, Ezra, Esther, Nehemiah, David, Paul, etc.). Fasting is the abstaining from nourishment for the sake of seeking the face of God! There is a normal fast and one that is called for a special event or a challenge to one's person or ministry. In Acts 13:2,3, the Early Church sent out Paul and Barnabas after fasting and prayer. Fasting is to be the normal part of a Christian life, just as giving and praying. Christ is our Model!

> *...**when** you **give** ... **when** you **pray** ... **when** you **fast**. (Matt. 6:3-4-8,16-18)*

> *Jesus said to them, "Can the friends of the bridegroom mourn as long as the bridegroom is with them? But the days will come when the bridegroom will be taken away from them, and then they will fast." (Matt 9:15-16)*

> *... the days will come ...when they shall fast. (Mark 2:20)*

> *One day as these men were worshiping the Lord and fasting, the Holy Spirit said, "Dedicate Barnabas and Saul for the special work to which I have called them." (Acts 13:2, NLT)*

## APPLICATION

Pentecost did nothing to lessen dependence on prayer. It only heightened the sense and need of prayer. The Early Church was a praying church and a missionary church and sent out Paul and Barnabas after fasting and prayer (Acts 1:14; 2:1-4; 3:3; 4:23-31; 6:3,4; 13:2,3). ***They continued steadfastly in the Apostle's doctrine and fellowship, and in breaking of bread, and in prayers (Acts 2:42).*** In Luke 11:5-13, a friend at comes at midnight with a desperate need and with persistence until he receives his request. In Luke 18:1-8, the widow petitions an unjust judge who gives what she requested. Jesus gives this parable with a lesson: ***Ask and it shall be given you; seek, and you shall find; knock, and it shall be opened unto you** (*Luke 18:1-8). In Acts 12:5,12 Peter is in prison and he prays. Jesus talks about the secret closet of prayer (Matt. 6:5-15).

Notice again the emphasis the Lord puts on prayer and world missions. Not only are we to pray for His Kingdom to be advanced, but we are called to pray for those laborers to proclaim His Kingdom to the world.

As you read this chapter, maybe you are one of those laborers. Is God calling you to be sent out to His harvest field? Do you feel that urge of the Spirit? Do you need to be ***kicked out*** from where you are to be a laborer in His harvest? When God has a man or woman, who is willing to labor for Him, He will accomplish His purpose in that person and in relationship to the Kingdom of God, first spiritually, not educationally. The Church needs laborers. It begins in prayer to the Lord of the Harvest, not in committees or just among Bible school graduates. Jesus called fishermen, tax collectors, political zealots, physicians, the quiet, the loud, sons of thunder, a doubter, and the unknown.

You might say, "But I am a nobody. There are others that are more qualified than I am." No, Jesus is teaching us the necessity of dependency, the recognition that we are incapable of doing anything by ourselves.

> *Glory only in the Lord for you see your calling, brethren, that not many wise according to the flesh, not many mighty, not many noble, are called. But God has chosen the foolish things of the world to put to shame the wise, and God has chosen the weak things of the world to put to shame the things which are mighty; and the base things of the world and the things which are despised God has chosen, and the things which are not, to bring to nothing the things that are, that no flesh should glory in His presence. But of Him you are in Christ Jesus, who became for*

*us wisdom from God — and righteousness and sanctification and redemption — that, as it is written, "He who glories, let him glory in the LORD." (I Cor. 1:26-31)*

*But we have this treasure in jars of clay to show that this all-surpassing power is from God and not from us. (II Cor. 4:7 NIV)*

God chooses the weak, what are considered foolish things in the natural because they recognize their weakness, their inability and their need to depend totally upon God, so that the Lord would get all the glory. God gets the glory when the world sees the power of God working through the vessels God chooses. That's us! Nobodies whom God has chosen to fill with His Spirit to reflect His glory to our world. The history of the Church testifies to this truth!

**Illustration**: Look at Gideon who was hiding from the Midianites, yet the Spirit of the Lord ***clothed Gideon*** and was called a ***mighty man of valor*** (Judges 6:12). He speaks to the Angel of the Lord, *I am the least in the tribe and the least in my family ... the youngest. (Jud. 6:15)* He goes on to say that *I am not sufficient for this task. I cannot do it.*

---

> "I am now, in 1864, waiting upon God for certain blessings, for which I have daily besought Him for 19 years and 6 months, without one day's intermission. Still the full answer is not yet given concerning the conversion of certain individuals. In the meantime, I have received many thousands of answers to prayer. I have also prayed daily, without intermission, for the conversion of other individuals about 10 years, for others about 18 months; and still the answer is not yet granted, concerning these persons [whom I have prayed for 19 years and 6 months]. Yet, I am daily continuing in prayer and expecting the answer. Be encouraged, dear Christian reader, with fresh earnestness to give yourself to prayer, if you can only be sure that you ask for things which are for the glory of God." (Note: He prayed for the conversion of one individual for 63 years. The person came to Christ at his funeral!)
>
> —George Mueller, *Autobiography*

Let our missions endeavors, our outreaches—those who we expect to witness to in our work, neighborhood, school—begin in prayer. Pray for the people the Lord would have you go and witness—for the prisons, for the universities, for God to stir up a hunger in the country, state, in your city of residence. Gather others to pray for the cities, a people group, or those the Lord would impress you with to share the Gospel. Begin in prayer! We have already stated that Jesus prayed in His lifetime. At His crucifixion He prayed, *"Father forgive them for they know not what they do."* Those coming to Christ today are a result of the prayers of Jesus in eternity and in time. Pray in season and out of season, in good times and bad times. Our life is to be a worship center for the Holy Spirit.

**Question:** What is our response? Will we pray and call out to God for those laborers and for those laboring in the harvest field? A specific harvest field? People groups? Will we be known not only for our preaching, but our praying as Jesus exemplified and commanded?

The Scripture says, *Pray in the Spirit on all occasions with all kinds of prayers and requests* (Eph. 6:18).

**Illustration:** Prayer is the mightiest force in the world. Some have not spent too much of their time in studying prayer—they *prayed!* Here are some examples from the Old Testament of those who, in bold, holy faith, pleaded with God and were heard.

## Biblically:

- Pharaoh was moved by the prayers of Moses.
- Artaxerxes was moved by the prayers of Nehemiah.
- Nebuchadnezzar was moved by the prayers of Daniel.
- Abraham prayed long for a son: Isaac came.
- Moses prayed: the Amalakites were destroyed.
- Hanna prayed (she was barren): Samuel was given to her.
- Elijah prayed: the heavens were shut and opened.
- Elisha prayed: drought came and also a dead child was resurrected.
- Hezekiah prayed: 185,100 Assyrians were slain.
- Daniel prayed: Archangels were set in motion in two kingdoms—Persia (Iran) and Greece.

## Historically:

- Savonarola prayed in Florence: a city was won for God.
- Martin Luther prayed: God broke the spell of ages.

- John Knox prayed: tyrants were terrified and Scotland was blessed.
- George Whitefield prayed: A thousand souls were saved in one day.
- George Mueller prayed: hungry orphans were fed.
- Hudson Taylor prayed: inland China was evangelized.

*Epaphras, who is one of yourselves, a servant of Christ Jesus, sends you greetings. [He is] always striving for you earnestly in his prayers, [pleading] that you may [as persons of ripe character and clear conviction] stand firm and mature [in spiritual growth], convinced and fully assured in everything willed by God. (Col. 4:12 AMP)*

**Conclusion:** God is seeking out intercessors.

*So, I sought for a man among them ... to stand in the gap before Me on behalf of the land, that I should not destroy it; but I found no one. (Ezekiel 22:30)*

***Moses:*** God was going to destroy the people of Israel and raise up another people for Moses to lead. Moses intercedes and reminds God of His past with the People of Israel (Ex. 32:7-14).

*So the Lord changed his mind about the terrible disaster he had threatened to bring on his people. (Ex 32:14, NLT)*

# Chapter Five

# Called—Sent

Jesus was called and sent by the Father to both Jews and Gentiles to fully identify with mankind. He was **called My Son out of Egypt** (Hosea 11:1; Matt. 2:15; John 1:1). **My meat is to do the will of Him that sent me** (John 4:34). **I have given them (the disciples) the words that You gave me** (17:8). **You have sent Me ... I have sent them into the world** (John 17:18). **The world has not known You, but I have known You and these [disciples] have known that You have sent Me** (John 17:25). **God sent forth His Son** (Gal. 4:4). He was sent to **give His life a ransom** (Matthew 20:28). He needed a body to die to fulfill the Old Testament type of animal sacrifices for sins. Jesus Christ now is the only Sacrifice needed. The Law for salvation is gone. We are now saved by grace. He came to **seek and to save that which was lost** (Luke 19:10). He came to serve, not to be served. He came to preach, save, heal, deliver, open up blinded eyes, to send out those who have experienced Christ, and to preach the *year of Jubilee* (Luke 4:19).

> *For I have given to them the words which You have given Me; and they have received them, and have known surely that I came forth from You; and they have believed that You sent Me. ... As You sent Me into the world, I also have sent them into the world. (John 17:8,18)*

> *Again he said, "Peace be with you. As the Father has sent me, so I am sending you (continuously). (John 20:21, NLT)*

Jesus Himself said **the Son can do nothing of Himself** (John 5:19). That is an amazing statement from Jesus, the Almighty Son of God! But when He came in the flesh, He limited Himself to be dependent upon the Father and the Holy Spirit to be an Example to us. He goes on to say that **I can do nothing on My own initiative ... I do only those things I see my Father do and say only what I hear my Father say** (John 5:30). He also said, **the Father in Me does His works** (John 14:10,25; 5:36). Jesus had an intimate relationship with His Father. He was teaching His disciples that intimacy with the Father was the key to everything He did (John 8:38).

Christ is our Model in dependence upon the Holy Spirit in our ministry. There is much we can do in the natural without the empowerment of the Holy Spirit. Spiritual results can only come with the enablement of the Holy Spirit. As Jesus depended upon His Father to speak His words and do His works, so Christ commands us to be recipients of the Spirit's anointing to speak and to do all that Jesus commands us to say and do. Jesus Christ obtained power for His divine works not by his inherent deity, but by His anointing through the Holy Spirit. He was subject to the same conditions as other men (John 14:13).

We have been **called out** from the world into His Kingdom (II Thess. 2:12). We are now **sent** back to the world from which we came, but are now not part of it. We have been sent to preach, heal, cast out devils, and even raise the dead (Matt. 10:8) ... ***As My Father has sent Me, even so send I you...***  (John 20:21).. We have been sent with His full authority and power to accomplish His mission. If those, to whom He has sent us, receive us, they receive Him. ***If they reject you, they reject Me***  (Luke 9:48; Matthew 10:16,40). He has **other sheep** (referring to the Gentiles) that *will* hear and believe the voice of the Shepherd through the voice of His messengers (John 10:27,28; 17:20,21). What a promise! What hope! We go with full assurance that there will be those who will hear and believe the Gospel! As He approached the end of His life, He said, ***Now, I am going to Him Who sent me*** (John 16:5). Again, His goal was to establish His Church in every people group worldwide.

His choice of followers did not come from seminaries, universities, Hollywood, or Wall Street. He chose a political zealot, a tax collector, a traitor, fishermen who were impulsive, the quiet, and the selfish. The disciples had internal bickering. What an encouragement to us. If He can work with them, He can work through us (I Cor. 1:26,27,29). His love for and view of persons was beyond the limit of logic, but very compatible with His nature. Jesus was sent by His heavenly Father to the world to fully identify with all of mankind. He came as the Servant of the Lord. He came to give His life a ransom. He came to serve, not to be served.

> *Then He appointed twelve, that they might be with Him and that He might send them out to preach ... (Mark 3:14)*

A priest once told me, while I was in seminary, this profound statement in the purpose of the Church: ***"to know Christ and make Him known!"***

The first calling of the disciples was first ***to Him***, not to ministry (Mark 3:14). In searching ten translations of the Bible, I find no phrase ***called to preach*** or ***called to ministry***. He ***sent them forth*** to preach many times (Mark 3:15; 6:7; Matt. 10:1; Luke 9:2; 10:1-11). Jesus said to Peter, **Follow Me and I WILL MAKE YOU fishers of men** (Matt. 4:19). He says to Peter and to us, "Make Me your soul's satisfaction, your priority in life and ministry, and your preeminence of love. **Follow Me** as Lord. I will do the making, the transforming, and will produce in and through you all My good pleasure … in that order!" (I Cor. 1:9; John 12:26). There was an immediate abandonment (Mark 1:17-19; Acts 9 – Paul; I Cor. 1:9). I will equip you and send you out (Mark 1:14). As we follow Christ, He gives us His heart for the purpose of His coming to earth. He loved to redeem. If we are to have the heart of Christ, we also are to weep for the lost. We need to be moved with compassion as Christ was. People are going to hell. We have the message to bring them redemption.

It is necessary that one continue to take "sabbaths." Jesus, following miracles and extensive ministry to the multitude, told His disciples to take a necessary break, not only to renew the body but also the spirit.

> *Then Jesus said, "Let's go off by ourselves to a quiet place and rest awhile." He said this because there were so many people coming and going that Jesus and his apostles didn't even have time to eat (Mark 6:31, NLT)*

Why? Because we all know people and preachers who are in ministry that they are doing the work of ministry, but their spirits are cold, they have left their first love, and they are lukewarm. Everything on the outside looks good, well respected by men. But God looks on the heart. They have left off intimacy with God and kept the outward demonstration of ministry. Intimacy with God is the priority calling of any minister of the Gospel!

Christ's goal was to establish a community of the King within every people group in the world capable of multiplying congregations of that entire people group into a fellowship of a local church. In His calling His disciples and us as well, He calls first to Himself, to intimacy, not to a place or ministry. Without intimacy with Him, the ministry becomes outward only where everything looks good on the outside, well respected of men. But God, who looks on the heart, sees it differently. The heart can become lukewarm or even cold! When we do not have active fellowship of intimacy with the Lord, our outward demonstration of ministry becomes a set of rules. The church in Ephesus had all the externals of ministry without intimacy with the Lord. They had *left their first love* (Rev. 2:4). Intimacy with God is the priority calling of any minister of the Gospel. Acts 4:31 demonstrates what happened when we have intimacy with Christ ...*they took notice of them that they had been with Jesus* (Luke 6:12-16; I Cor. 1:26-3).

Jesus Himself is our Example, as said in John 5:19: *"the Son can do nothing of Himself."* That is an amazing statement from Jesus, the Almighty Son of God! But when He came in the flesh, He limited Himself to be dependent upon the Father and the Holy Spirit, to be an Example to us. He goes on to say in John 5:30: *"I can do nothing on My own initiative ... I do only those things I see my Father do and say only what I hear my Father say."* He also said, *The Father in ME does His works* (John 14:10). Jesus had an intimate relationship with His Father. He was teaching His disciples that intimacy with the Father was the key to everything He did.

Jesus transfers His Kingdom message to His apostles to finish its mission of making disciples of <u>all nations</u>. Jesus, speaking to His Father, says, *"I have brought You glory on earth by completing the work You gave Me do to"* (John 17:4). Jesus completed His assignment. The Church must <u>and</u> will complete its assignment also.

## **CALLING OF THE DISCIPLES**

- Simon the Canaanite — called the zealot (Luke 6:15)
- James and John — "sons of thunder" who became leaders in the church; John called the apostle of love (Matt. 4:21; Mark 1:20)
- Matthew — the publican and tax collector
- Andrew — quiet (Matt. 4:19; Mark 1:17)
- Peter — rash, impetuous (Matt. 10:2; John 1:42). He curses and denies the Lord, yet, he becomes the preacher at Pentecost 10 days later! (John 21:19,20)
- Thaddeus — not much spoken of him (Mark 3:18)
- Phillip — John 1:43
- Thomas — doubter (John 20:24-29)
- Bartholomew — (Matt. 10:3)
- Simon — fisherman (Matt. 4:18)
- Judas — son of James (Luke 6:15) [9]
- Judas — the betrayer and fulfillment of prophecy - (Matt. 10:4)

---

[9] I Cor. 1:9; John 15:16,17

Jesus has that authority that when we hear His voice, He gives us the desire and the power to follow Him. We submit ourselves to the Lordship of Christ when we respond to the call to follow Him. He is not only Savior, but He is Lord. He owns us with absolute authority yet with such tender love and compassion. He wants the best for His glory and for our good. He is sovereign. *When I submit to His loving Lordship, I make Him happy. And I am the happiest when I make Him happy!*

The choice is the Lord's, not man's. We are not an accident with God. We have been *chosen out of the world before the foundation of the world* (Eph. 1:4; John 15:19; 17:20). He has specifically placed us where we are in the vine in our lives and ministry.

> *Then He appointed twelve, that they might be with Him and that He might send them out to preach ... (Mark 3:14)*

Now Jesus is saying the same to His disciples. *Apart from Me you can do nothing* (John 15:5). Apart from Christ, there can be no spiritual results of our labors and mission. Again, the reason is that we can *"do"* ministry without intimacy, without a heart of worship and dependency upon the Lord. Our "ministry" becomes mechanical, legalistic, without joy, and without the full blessings of Christ (Rev. 2:1-4). A statistic in America is staggering: "Only one person out of every 10 who enters the ministry will still be in it when he reaches the age of 65!" (John Maxwell, *The Twenty-One Most Powerful Minutes in a Leader's Day*). That is a 90% drop-out rate! I am sure there is more than one reason, but one can safely say that a majority either did not have the call or that they were what we call *"burned out"*... they were doing the ministry without the inner resource of the Holy Spirit to help them. They lost touch with Christ who is able to give them the strength and grace to continue. We have failed to take our "sabbath" rests.

Again, Jesus says to us, *Abide in Me, and I in you ... If you abide in Me, and My words abide in you, ask whatever you wish, and it will be done for you* (John 15:4,7). Results of abiding and keeping the commandments of the Lord are **answered prayer** (v. 7), **fruitfulness** (v. 8), and **joy** (v. 11)! When we do not bear fruit, the Husbandman prunes us that we might bear more fruit.

It is what Psalm 37:4 says, *Delight yourself in the Lord, and He will give you the desires of your heart.* Psalm 37:23 says, *The steps of a good man are ordained of the Lord, WHEN He delights in His way.* We do the delighting. He does the ordaining ... in that order. We are to *follow in His steps* (I Pet. 1:21), to be dependent upon Him for His mission, whether around the world, next door, or in our workplace. *He who abides in Him ought himself to walk as His walked* (I John 1:3-6; 2:4-6; 4:8). It means to love what God loves and hate what God hates—what fellowship has light with darkness? (II Cor. 6:14) If we are not in agreement with Him, not keeping His commandments, if we are not walking the way He walked, then we cannot have a true relationship. We do not know Him (Matt. 7:23; I John 2:4). It is Jesus who said,

> *Abide in Me, and I in you. As the branch cannot bear fruit of itself, unless it abides in the vine, neither can you, unless you abide in Me. ... If you abide in Me, and My words abide in you, you will ask what you desire, and it shall be done for you. (John 15:4,7)*

We abide in Him when we walk in the light, we do not practice and enjoy sinning, we keep His commandments, and we do not love the world. It is so important in ministry to maintain an intimacy with God in worship, experiencing and obeying the Word of God, fasting, prayer, and expressed faith. Love for Christ finds the time! Satan would distract us from having intimacy with the Lord. We must discipline ourselves with the help of the Holy Spirit. We must deny ourselves, take up the cross, and follow Him (I John 1:3-6; 2:1,4-6,10,15).

> *...friendship with the world is enmity with God. (James 4:4)*

> *... what fellowship has light with darkness? (II Cor. 6:14; I John 3:6,24)*

The Lord called His disciples in the "workplace." *They left all and followed Him* (Mark 1:17,18; Luke 5:10,27; Matt. 4:19; John 1:39). He called James and John while they were mending their nets. *They immediately left their father, their nets, their hired servants and went after Him* (Mark 1:19, 20). The Lord called Matthew while he was collecting taxes. *He arose, and followed Him* (Matt. 9:9). He called Paul, *an apostle called and set apart for the Gospel of God* (Rom. 1:1; Gal. 1:1). Jesus has that authority that when we hear His voice, He gives us the power to follow Him. We submit ourselves to the Lordship of Christ when we respond to the call. He is not only Savior but Lord. He owns us with such tender love and compassion and wants the best for His glory and for our good. He is sovereign. *When I submit to His Lordship I make Him happy. When I do, I am the happiest!*

As we look at the calling of the disciples, we are awestruck at His choices. Simon was a political right-wing zealot. James and John were called *sons of*

***thunder*** who were power hungry for higher positions in the Kingdom. They later became leaders of the Church and John (the apostle of love – Matt. 4:21; Mark 1:20) wrote the last book of the Bible. Andrew was quiet (Matt. 4:19; Mark 1:17) and Thomas was a doubter. All the disciples forsook Him. Peter curses and denies the Lord, yet becomes a preacher at Pentecost ten days later (John 21:19, 22). Not much is said of Thaddeus. Then there is Phillip and Paul, a persecutor of the Church and a religious zealot! Matthew was a tax collector.

In the Old Testament we have other examples of God's calling. Again, look at who God has called. **Abraham** lied. **Moses** was a murderer. **David** was an adulterer and a murderer. Then there are you and I! It was and is the grace and the Spirit of God to make these powerful vessels for His glory!

God makes no mistakes in His choices, many unknown by name. He chose Hur, the only place in the Bible he is mentioned, who held up the hands of Moses. It was Naman's little maid who encouraged him to obey the prophet. No name given. The four men who let down from the roof to be healed by the Lord. Then there were the men who let Paul down from the wall and spared his life. Again, no name given yet critical in the sparing of Paul's life who wrote nearly two-thirds of the New Testament. There were women who ministered unto Him of their substance—unnamed (Luke 8:1-3). In I Corinthians 12:28, the Scripture speaks of ***"helps."*** They are listed with the apostles and prophets, which are more visible. In I Samuel 30, those who stayed by the stuff reaped the results of the victory as much as those who were in the frontlines of the battle.

## Chapter Six

# The Great Commission[10]

Jesus gave what was commanded to the Church. ***Preach the Gospel*** in Mark 16:15 – ***Go into all the world and preach the gospel to every creature ... signs shall follow, there will be tongues, and you shall cast out demons.*** The Gospel is not only the ***truth of God*** (Col. 1:5), it is also the ***power of God*** (Rom. 1:16). Jesus' command to His disciples to ***disciple the nations*** was not an option. His mandate is clear: ***as His Father sent Me (to the world), so send I you*** (John 20:21). As the Head of the Church and Lord of the Harvest, and the King of all nations, He has the right and the authority to send His disciples to carry the Gospel message to the ends of the earth. Christ sends us to the world with the same mission. His field was the world ... ***that all men should come into the knowledge of the truth*** (I Tim. 2:4). Jesus was sent by His ***Father to be the Savior of the whole world*** **(I John 4:14). That He would draw all men to Himself** (John 12:32), ***and this Gospel of the Kingdom must be first preached in the world, and then the end shall come ... to every creature ... and to make disciples of all nations*** (Matt. 24:14; Mark 16:15; Matt. 28:19).

Jesus' mandate was to the whole world, not just a select group of people but from every strata of society, the rich and the poor, the outcasts and those in high levels in society, to political leaders, to women, to children (He ***blessed*** them), to individuals and to the masses, and to the sick and the hungry needing a miracle. His saving grace did not leave anyone out of His outreach to them. He compelled them with His preaching the Kingdom of God, with His miracles, with His love and compassion, with His consistency, with His uncompromising truth yet with His overwhelming love to the lost, ***the good and the bad***.

Jesus gave the invitation to the multitudes long before He gave the Great Commission to the disciples. His invitation was to ***come unto Me and***

---

[10] John 10:16; Matt. 28:18-20; Mark 16:15; Luke 24:47-49; John 20:21; Acts 1:8

***I will give you rest*** (Matt. 11:28). This verse cannot be separated from the next two verses. He called **to *take up My yoke, and learn of Me for I am meek and lowly of heart*** (Matt. 11:29,30). What Jesus did while on earth: He preached, healed, cast out devils, raised the dead and <u>discipled</u> His hearers, especially His disciples. He modeled what He commanded His disciples to do upon leaving earth ... to ***make disciples***, not only in His teaching, but His giving them ministry assignments, continual interaction of encouragement, correction, rebuke, and identifying with them in every way.

When the Church responds to the **Great Commission** (Matt. 28:19,20), it is being sent to ***all nations*** given to Christ in answer to His prayer before time. This was the purpose God had in Genesis. The same commission was explained to Abram: ***I will bless all nations through you*** (Gen. 12:2). God sees the Church as a partner in establishing His Kingdom. When we see the price of Redemption on the Cross for the world, we will have a worldwide vision.

We need to go to the younger generation, the university students, political leaders, to the military, schools, neighbors, and orthodox churches, in the streets and in the marketplace. We need frontier missionaries to go to people normally out of reach of society. We need to share the Gospel with them. Piety is not enough. Sincerity is not enough. Goodness is not enough. Salvation only comes through Jesus Christ! (Acts 4:12; Rom. 10:13)

> ...***as you are going*** *[in the original] into all the world and preaching ["make disciples" in the original] the Gospel ... (Mark 16:15)*
>
> *... baptizing [evangelism] and teaching them to do whatsoever I have commanded you ... to all nations ... (Luke 24:47)*
>
> *...compel them to come in ... [drag them in] (Luke 14:23, MSG)*
>
> "Go out into the busiest intersections in town and invite anyone you find to the banquet." The servants went out on the streets and rounded up everyone they laid eyes on, good and bad, regardless. And so the banquet was on — every place filled. (Matt 22:9,10, MSG)

---

**HIS PROMISE:** *"and lo, I am with you even unto the end of the age."*

---

We are not alone in our obedience to the Great Commission. Before Jesus left His disciples, He gave them (and us) some staggering promises:

*Most assuredly, I say to you, he who believes in Me, the works that I do he will do also; and greater works than these he will do, because I go to My Father. (John 14:12)*

*Teach these new disciples to obey all the commands I have given you. And be sure of this: I am with you always, even to the end of the age. (Matt. 28:20, NLT)*

## ILLUSTRATION

This story is told from the Salvation Army. Several ladies went to London. They were running into many obstacles. The people did not care, the message was not received, and they did everything they knew to do. They sent a telegram to William Booth, founder of the Salvation Army, saying that they had tried everything and nothing was working. His response was in two words: "<u>Try tears.</u>" When all else fails, try tears. Allow God to break us and see what He can do in our mission field to our neighbors, cities, and the nation! What about the lost?

Jesus' last command was to go to preach and heal. It was not about personal welfare, houses, or health. His concern was for the lost. He called His disciples to be with Him and to send them forth. It is what we call the Great Commission. He gives us the honor and privilege by God to share Him with others! Jesus goes before us in prayer. Other sheep that I have **will hear My voice** (John 10:16; 17:20). He goes before us in prayer in the person of the Holy Spirit (Heb. 7:25). It is the Holy Spirit that brings the ultimate results, not just the command to go (John 15:26,27; 16:8-15). Christ is sending His disciples for the same purpose the Father sent Him into the world. The mandate for missions does not ultimately rest on the command of the Great Commission, but the presence and power of the Holy Spirit.

*As You sent Me into the world, I also have sent them into the world. (John 17:18)*

***I sent you to reap where you did not sow*** ...(John 4:38; 20:21). ***Christ in you the Hope of glory*** *(Col. 1:27).* Christ lives in the Church. Christ works through the Church (Mark16:20); with all authority in heaven and earth (Matt. 28:18). Christ goes before us in prayer and in the Person of the Spirit (Heb. 7:25). All results are the work of the Holy Spirit, not just a command to fulfill (John 15:26,27; 16:8-15). Jesus <u>prays</u> for His disciples (John 17:9,15), <u>sends</u> them into the world (John 17:18), <u>sanctifies</u> Self so that the disciples would be sanctified (John 17:19). There are 270 references of the term *disciples* in the Gospels and Acts. The Epistles have replaced the term with *saints*. To make disciples is modeled by Jesus' example. He said, **Follow Me ... come after Me....**

Jesus walked, ate, and lived with His disciples. He gave them preaching and ministry assignments, with follow-up.

- Prayed with and for them
- Taught them aside, besides the multitudes
- Encouraged and corrected them, both individually and collectively
- Washed their feet as a Servant
- Selected three to go with Him on the mount, who would then be leaders in the Church
- Gave them the same challenges that He gave to the people, challenged them to be a follower of Him, to deny self, take up the Cross, and follow Him
- He valued all souls. He was as much interested in the one lost sheep as He was in the ninety and nine.
- He continually reminded them that He came to do the will of His Father, to speak His words, and to do His works.

He modeled what He commanded His disciples to do: *make disciples!*

Jesus commissioned His disciples. He sends His disciples with power and authority to accomplish the mission. Jesus had been given all authority by the Father. *You have given Him authority over all flesh. He then He called His twelve disciples together and gave them power and authority over all demons, and to cure diseases* (Matt. 28:18; Eph. 1:20-22; Luke 9:1; Acts 2:36). Authority is His (John 14:12-14; 16:23,24). Based on the authority in the resurrected Christ, go to all nations. They are subjects of Christ's Kingdom (Mark 16:15). He opens and shuts. All closed doors are open to Him (Rev. 3:7).

## AS YOU ARE GOING ... (MATT. 28:18)

Christ is the Head of the Church (Eph. 1:10; 3:10; Col. 1:17,18) and He commands His church to GO. Interestingly, **"go"** is *not the command* **of the Great Commission.** Literally, in the Greek, the phrase is in the *present aorist participle*—*having gone ... as you are going ... make disciples* (Matt. 28:18). They had already been sent in the past. Keep going, keep doing what I sent you to do while I was here on earth. Continue going when I leave. The Holy Spirit will by your Enabler and Power. I will no longer be with you, but the Holy Spirit will be your Power. *You shall be witnesses ...* (Acts 1:8). Jesus took for granted that they would be scattered with the empowerment of the Holy Spirit and with the persecution He predicted (Acts 8:4; 11:19-21). The command is to *disciple the nations* with evangelism (baptism) and *teaching them to observe ALL that I have commanded you.* Christ is sending His disciples for the same purpose the Father sent Him into the world. Because I have all power and authority, go and make disciples, do not just preach and heal. Jesus knew that after the baptism in the Holy Spirit, the Spirit would send them to the world. They had been going with Him while He was on earth. Christ was no longer present with them, but the Holy Spirit was given in His place. He would be their Power (John 14:12-15; 16:13,14). Christ would be sending them in His Name with the Gospel. Keep going as you did in the past three and a half years with the same power you had when I was present with you.

When Jesus commissioned His disciples, He sent His disciples with power and authority to accomplish the mission. Jesus had been given all authority by the Father. *You have given Him authority over all flesh. He then He called His twelve disciples together and gave them power and authority over all demons, and to cure diseases* (Matt. 28:18; Eph. 1:20-22; Luke 9:1; Acts 2:36; John 14:12-14; 16:23,24). Based on Christ's authority in the resurrected Christ, go to "all nations." They are subjects of Christ's Kingdom (Mark 16:15). He opens and shuts. All closed doors are open to Him (Rev. 3:7).

In Matt. 28:18, the Lord says, *All authority has been given to Me in heaven and on earth ... as you are going, make disciples* ... because I command you ... because I have all authority and I have given it to you ... *going* because I have all power and have given you that power to fulfill My word ... because I go before you ... *going* because I have come to redeem the world and they need to hear the Gospel ... *going* because I have prayed and am praying for you ... *going* because I am praying for those who shall believe on Me through your word ... *going* because you shall receive the reward of your labor ... going because you love the Lord and want to please Him in all things ... going because you want to see more worshipers of God ... going because those who are filled with the Spirit will have a missionary spirit to preach the Gospel around the world, to all people groups (Mark 16:15). There are still many unreached people groups that have yet to hear the Gospel. These should be the target of missionary outreach!

*As you are going*, I am authorizing you as My delegates. I am giving you authority. Jesus said to use **My Name** ... *and lo I am with you, even to the*

***very end of the age to all nations*** ...the Name that is above all names and with all power. Jesus gave us a signed check. We need to fill in the blanks that are in agreement with His will. Satan has no authority to dominate the Christian church. God has delivered us from fear, from the power and authority of darkness. We have been translated into the Kingdom of His dear Son.

Jesus took for granted they would be scattered when they were baptized in the Holy Spirit. There would be persecution (***they were scattered everywhere preaching the Word,*** Acts 8:4; ***now they which were scattered abroad upon the persecution, preaching the Word,*** Acts 11:19-21.) It was already happening with Christ. He was received and rejected. They had been sent in the past—continue going when I leave. Continue to have miracles. I want you to go in my Name (John 14:12-15). Keep going, keep doing what I sent you to do while I was here on earth. Again he said, **Peace be with you. As the Father has sent me, so I am sending you** (John 20:21, NLT).

He was sending them to all nations (Rev. 5:9; 7:9,10; Luke 24:45-47; John 11:52). The nations are to discipled and taught to observe all kingdom regulations, ***everything I have commanded you*** (Matt. 28:19; cf. Matt. 5-7).

## **MAKE DISCIPLES (IMPERATIVE)**

This verse is a command to ***make disciples***. You do the following, I will make you—train and develop you—as My disciple so that you can disciple others. Your goal is to have those to whom we speak and teach become followers of Jesus, to become His pupil, His disciple. We witness regularly. Sometimes we see the person one time. The long-term mission of the church is to make a community of believers followers of Christ, not just converts where Jesus is Lord. It is to establish a Church that Christ is building, a fellowship of believers, and to have a self-governing, self-supporting, and self-propagating Church. When we follow Jesus as our Model for missions, we are to teach, train, and make followers of Christ, not primarily program our church members, but see in them the very image and likeness of Christ Himself. ***But you have not so learned Christ*** (Eph. 4:20). The goal is that followers become the ***likeness of Christ***, not doctrines about Him. Jesus always had 12 disciples, though He preached to the multitudes. He had three that He took up to the mount, and then He had John who leaned on Jesus' breast.

Jesus' command to ***make disciples of all nations*** involves people going to all nations. We are to follow His pattern in Matt. 4:19—***follow Me and I will make ... not evangelism*** only. How can people make disciples of all nations unless they go to all nations? Here are the Church's marching orders! When you go, make disciples!

The call of Christ is for believers to *be His disciples*. The demands Jesus made to become a disciple are very clear to every believer. Not only is He to be my Savior, but also my **LORD**. In II Peter 2:1, the term *Lord* in the original is *"despotes."* The meaning is obvious. Jesus is called a despot! However, the difference between despots as know we them today and who Jesus is totally different. He is a loving despot, all-wise, good, kind, merciful, holy, righteous, merciful, full of grace, etc. There is no salvation without Lordship (Matt. 16:24; Luke 9:23,57-60; 14:27; Mark 8:34; John 12:26; Eph. 5:1)! Literally, Jesus must be Lord, and no other loves must come before our love for Him.

> *If you love your father or mother more than you love me, you are not worthy of being mine; or if you love your son or daughter more than me, you are not worthy of being mine. If you refuse to take up your cross and follow me, you are not worthy of being mine. If you cling to your life, you will lose it; but if you give up your life for me, you will find it. (Matt 10:37-39, NLT)*

What is a disciple? A disciple is a person who receives Jesus Christ as Savior, and follows Him as Lord of his or her life. It means to **take up the (His) Cross and follow Me** (Mark 8:34). It means sacrifice. The claims of Christ come first. Then a disciples' life finds true joy and peace with God. A disciple is one who makes Christ Lord over all relationships, ambitions, and over all one's possessions. He gave specific criteria for a true disciple.

The church is not to win converts (souls), to a denomination, or to make them church members, but to Christ Himself as Savior and Lord, the impartation of His nature, integrity and character. This is not confined to Israel, but to all nations—the entire world by Christ's right of creation (John 1:3) and redemption (John 3:17), internationally, interracially, and intercultural.

> *"If anyone comes to Me and does not hate his father and mother, wife and children, brothers and sisters, yes, and his own life also, he cannot be My disciple. And whoever does not bear his cross and come after Me cannot be My disciple. ... So likewise, whoever of you does not forsake all that he has cannot be My disciple. (Luke 14:26,27,33)*[11]

---

[11] John 13:35; 15:8; 20:21; Mark 11:17

Jesus gives us other practical criteria of discerning true disciples (John 8:31,32).

> *If someone claims, "I know God," but doesn't obey God's commandments, that person is a liar and is not living in the truth. But those who obey God's word truly show how completely they love him. That is how we know we are living in him. (1 John 2:4,5, NLT)*

## ALL NATIONS

> *... and that repentance and remission of sins should be preached in His name to all nations, beginning at Jerusalem. (Luke 24:47)*

Note: When Jesus was referring to **all nations** in the Great Commission, He may have been referring to these Old Testament passages concerning the missionary vision for His people. (See Gen. 18:18; 22:18; 26:4; Psa. 48:2; 71:11,17; 81:18; 85:9; 116:1; Isa. 2:2; 25:76; 52:10; 56:7; 61:11; 66:18-20.)

This command is ***going into all the world and preach the Gospel to every creature*** (Mark 16:15).

- To all people groups—all people groups need to hear the Gospel.
- 91% of all Christian outreach/evangelism targets those countries where at least 60% of their population is considered a Christian nation.

This is easily demonstrated by looking at some statistics concerning missions. Only one percent of the church's entire missionary force is ministering to Muslims. This means that there is about one Christian missionary for every one million Muslims. The church has more missionaries working among Alaska's 400,000 residents than in the entire Muslim world! (This is according to the *Arabic Bible*, a ministry to the Islamic world.)

> *... as the Father has sent me, even so send I you ... as You (Father) sent Me into the world, I am sending you into the world. (John 17:18)*

> *And other sheep I have which are not of this fold; them also I must bring, and they will hear My voice; and there will be one flock and one shepherd. (John 10:16)*

The Commission does not say to go when your plans are complete. **Definition**: *"A disciple is a believing person living a life of conscious and constant* *identification with the Lord in life, death and resurrection through words, behavior, attitudes, motives and purpose, fully realizing Christ's absolute ownership of his life, joyfully embracing Christ as Savior, delighting in the lordship of Christ, and living by abiding, indwelling resources of Christ according to the imprinted pattern and purpose of Christ for the chief end of glorifying his Lord and Savior..."* (Peters, pp. 187-188).

We are His ambassadors (II Cor. 5:20), invested with His power (Acts 1:8; 3:12-16), and authorized to use His Name (Acts 3:6; 4:10). To teach and to train up and make students and followers of Christ—not only methods, but Christ Himself (Luke 14:25-33)!

## BAPTIZING & TEACHING

These are participles and not commands. They are together in the command of Christ to make disciples and not to be separated. How do you *make disciples?*

### A. EVANGELISM

By sharing the Gospel on the streets, neighborhoods, churches, crusades, outreaches, and at our workplace by also showing the compassion of Christ in practical ways and sharing Him with those with whom you work. It is a radical break from the past and openly confessing Jesus Christ as Lord.

There is a difference between evangelism and missions. Evangelism may be personal and one time, while missions is more permanent. The goal is to establish a body of believers. It includes evangelism in its outreach and discipling in its continuing ministry. Billy Graham evangelistic meetings usually spend two years in preparation with churches. Twenty-one people began attending the church we pastored after a Billy Graham crusade in Oakland.

### B. WATER BAPTISM

The New Testament knows nothing of *secret* believers—***confess me openly before men*** (Matthew 10:26-33). New Testament believers were publicly baptized in water. It is openly identifying with Jesus Christ. Of course, there are some modifications in restricted countries. The open baptism may not be in public, but with only a few. The household of Cornelius believed and was baptized (Acts 10:46-48). The Eunuch from Ethiopia believed and was baptized by Philip (Acts 8:36-39). The Ephesians believed and were baptized (Acts 19:5).

## THREE BAPTISMS

1. Body – I Cor. 12:12; Eph. 4:4; Gal. 3:2;7,28; I Cor. 6:17
2. Water — Matt. 28:19; Acts 2:38,39
3. Spirit – Acts 1:5,6,8; 2:43; Mark 16:17

## TEACHING (INSTRUCTION):

To continue in the teachings of Christ, we are to be instructing at all levels in a church, from children, to teenagers, to adults and all levels of ministry from the singles, married, and all others, from all people groups, nationalities, and races. It is a lifelong process depending on the Word and the Spirit with God-inspired teachers to help us grow. As followers of Christ and leaders, we are challenged to teach as well as preach.

> *Jesus said to the people who believed in him, "You are truly my disciples if you remain faithful to my teachings. And you will know the truth, and the truth will set you free." (John 8:31, NLT)*
>
> *He (the Holy Spirit) will guide you into all Truth ... (John 16:13)*
>
> *... they continued in the apostles' teaching ... (Acts 2:42)*
>
> *... warning every man and teaching every man in all wisdom ... (Col. 1:28)*

## <u>ALL THAT JESUS HAD COMMANDED</u>

Jesus' words are ***Spirit and Life*** *(*John 6:63).

The foundation of the *house* must be established on ***the sayings of Mine*** (Matt. 7:24-27). To have a solid foundation, one must include all the sayings of Christ. This is more than John 3:16, but also includes the *hard sayings* of Christ—repentance, denying of self, selling all that you have, loving Christ more than family or position, taking up the Cross and following Christ as Savior and Lord. We are to teach not only the Parable of the Prodigal Son in Luke 15:11-32, but also the parable of the Last Judgment in Matthew 35:31-46! We are to teach about sin, repentance, death, judgment, and hell, as well as grace, forgiveness, love, heaven, and eternal life. Christ does not give us the option or the right to pick and choose, if we are to model Jesus and obey His commandment *to* ***teach all things whatsoever I have commanded you.***

To be truly *"**visitor-friendly**"* is to speak the whole truth in love. The Lordship of Christ demands complete allegiance, truths that are eternal and His absolute claims. He is the King of Truth and always speaks with authority, yet it is always with GRACE. Jesus taught absolutes, yet was very kind and patient with His disciples' unbelief, arrogance, rivalry for position, and others not following Him. It is important to teach the books of the Bible, not just topics. One needs also to teach spiritual as well as practical matters of the personal life at home and at work from a Biblical perspective. It is always a challenge to teach all that Jesus commanded. There is a need to teach about the gifts and ministries of the Body of Christ, the gifts of the Spirit, defense of the Gospel, and train and release the members of the Body for ministry.

Otherwise, we have a weak foundation and are giving partial truth and no real salvation or full Gospel! When we communicate truth in the right spirit of love and compassion and in the right time, the Holy Spirit takes truth and applies it. The soil and the response to the seed we leave with the Holy Spirit. All teaching is to be done with *love and grace*. Jesus taught absolutes, yet was very kind and patient with His disciples' unbelief, arrogance, of others not following, and rivalry for position, etc. (Mark 9:43-48).

> *If you love your father or mother more than you love me, you are not worthy of being mine; or if you love your son or daughter more than me, you are not worthy of being mine. If you refuse to take up your cross and follow me, you are not worthy of being mine. If you cling to your life, you will lose it; but if you give up your life for me, you will find it. (Matt 10:37-39, NLT)*

## AND LO I AM WITH YOU

Hallelujah! With such a command to disciple the nations, we need the Presence and Power of Christ with His command and His authority. We go with Him who is going before us. We pray that His Kingdom would come as we go. He has already prepared the ground for those who will hear and knows those who will not hear, but reject the Message (Mark 16:20; I Cor. 3:9).

## APPLICATION

God has made redemption available to all peoples, without exceptions. The challenge to the church is to preach the Gospel to the unreached of our world. Today, those in missions estimate that 90% of missionaries work in 94% of already reached peoples of the world. The 10-40 window has the most unreached people in world. Jesus the Model Missionary asks us to identify with the culture without loss of identity, to enter into other people's worlds, as Christ did with us, without compromising our Christian conviction, values or standards. The Lord is asking us not to take away the culture or change it unless it violates Scripture, for example, song, dress, mannerisms, family, etc. There is not a form or practice that is a requirement for entrance into the Christian community, except repentance, faith in Jesus Christ, and walking in obedience to Him. We need to respect culture without compromising Biblical Truth.

# CHAPTER SEVEN

# Authority[12]

Following Jesus in mission, one must have authority. Jesus came to earth as the Son of God and the Son of Man with full authority and power to accomplish His mission in the power of the Holy Spirit. Jesus had the same authority as His Father (John 10:25-30). As God and Creator, He has absolute and unconditional sovereignty and authority over the whole world and its inhabitants. God, who has absolute and unconditional authority, gave this same authority to His Son: ... *the Father has given him all judgment and authority* (John 10:20-25; 5:22,27; Ephesians 1:20,23; Hebrews 2:7,9; Mark 6:7; Luke 10:19; Matt. 10:1; 28:18; Luke 5:24). He had authority to forgive sins (Mark 2:10; Luke 5:24) *Your sins are forgiven* (John 5:25,26). *Christ is the Head of all and rules with absolute authority over all* (Col. 2:10; I Peter 3:22; I Cor. 15:24; Revelation 12:10). His teaching and His miraculous works were in power and with authority with the people responding. They were *astonished at His teaching... He taught them as one having authority* (Matt. 7:28,29; Mark 1:22; 11:28,29,33; Luke 4:36; 8:27; John 5:22). He had power to *give eternal life* (John 17:2). He also had power over the unseen world of the devil and demons (Mark 5:12; Luke 8:33; Matthew 17:15-21). He also had authority and power over sin (Mark 2:3-12 – the palsied man). When He commissioned His disciples *He gave them authority and power over unclean spirits* (Mark 6:7), over nature (*Jesus rebuked the winds*, Mark 4:39), healing all kinds of diseases (Mark 1:34; 3:10), and even at death He could have called twelve legions of angels (Matthew 26:53). There were not limitations to His authority. *All authority has been given to Me in heaven and on earth (Matt. 28:18).* We are authorized to use His Name and by His power to proclaim the Gospel with some astonishing results.

---

[12] "A person's right to do certain things because of the position or office he holds." (See Psa. 29:10.)

The disciples (and we) were given authority to use His Name in prayer (John 14:13-15; 16:23). His Name was used to bring about healing (Acts 3:16; 4:7), deliverance (Acts 16:18), and salvation (Acts 4:12). Jesus derived His authority from one other Source.

## SCRIPTURES

Jesus' other authority was the Scriptures. *This day is the Scripture fulfilled* (Luke 4:21). Jesus is the living Word (John 1:14). In Matt. 4:4,7,10 at His temptation, He quotes the word—*it is written* (Matt. 4:4, 7). In John 2:22, *they believed the Scripture and the word that Jesus had spoken.* Notice the Scripture and the Word of Jesus are the same. Jesus began His ministry with the Scriptures: *It is written* (Luke 4:1-11). Satan responds: "Has God said?" *My words are Spirit and Life ...* (John 6:63). They testify of Christ.

> *In the beginning the Word already existed. The Word was with God, and the Word was God. He existed in the beginning with God. God created everything through him, and nothing was created except through him. (John 1:1-3, NLT)*

Jesus on the road to Emmaus spoke to them of the Scriptures. *He opened their understanding that they might understand the Scripture* (Luke 24:25,32,44-48). *The disciples believed the Scripture* (John 2:22). -; search the Scriptures—*they speak about Me (John* 5:39). *He that believes on Me as the Scriptures has said* (John 7:38). *Hath not the Scripture said?* (John 5:42) *That the Scripture might be fulfilled* (John 19:24). *That the Scripture might be fulfilled* (John 19:36). *Which he promised before by His prophets in the holy Scriptures* (Romans 1:2).

## NOTE

Over 300 times He is prophesied in the Old Testament. Jesus came to fulfill the Scriptures (Matthew 26:54; 13:14; Mark 15:28; Luke 22:37; John 17:12). The disciples were given power and authority when they were sent out by the Lord to preach the Gospel, heal the sick and all manner of diseases, and cast out demons (Matthew 10:1; Mark 3:15; 6:7; Luke 9:1; 10:1). After His resurrection, Jesus commissioned them with the same authority and power He gave them while He was on earth (Matt. 28:18-20; Luke 24:24-49; John 20:21). He also commissioned them to preach the Gospel and said that in His Name they would do mighty works (Mark 16:15-18). In the Book of

Acts, *they went everywhere preaching the Word* (Acts 4:31; 6:2,4; 8:4,25,35; 10:37,44; 15:7; 11:1,19; 12:24; 17:11; 19:20; et al). When we preach the Word, we preach Christ, for He is the living Word, born of the Spirit, anointed by the Spirit, and His words are Spirit and life (John 6:63). When we preach Christ, we preach the Gospel (Acts 8:4,5). When we preach the Gospel, we preach Christ, for He is the living Word, born of the Spirit, anointed by the Spirit, and His words are spirit and life. The disciples were shocked that *even demons are subject to us in Your Name* (Luke 10:12). Jesus cautioned them that they were not to rejoice in that truth and reality, *but rather rejoice because your names are written in heaven.*

## SCRIPTURES AND THE SPIRIT

There is no separation. The Bible is a missionary book. Jesus said, *My words are Spirit and life* (Luke 6:63). The Scriptures testify of Christ. The first message of Peter was from the Scriptures: *This is that which was spoken by the prophet Joel* (Acts 2:16). James says that Gentiles are coming to faith in Jesus Christ as a fulfillment of prophecy (Amos 9:11,12). Jesus used the Scriptures in the Temptation (Matt. 4:4 – *it is written*, Luke 4:1-11). Satan questions with his response, *Hath God said?* The Word becomes a reality by the power of the Holy Spirit—the Spirit's inspiration. Peter, in Acts 2:16, said, *This is that which was spoken by the prophet Joel.* The message was a prophecy from Joel. James says Gentiles coming to faith in Jesus Christ is a fulfillment of the prophecy of Amos 9:11,12; *And the Word of God continued to increase* (Acts 6:7). *The Word increased* (Acts 12:24). *The Word of the Lord was spreading* (Acts 13:49). *The Word of the Lord continued to increase and prevail mightily* (Acts 19:20). Jesus said, *My word shall not pass away* (Mark 13:31; Matt. 24:35). They estimate there are 100-130 million Chinese Christians—all without missionaries—but they have the Word of God. Billy Graham in his evangelistic messages oftentimes reads or quotes 20 to 30 verses in a single message!

> *Then the word of God spread, and the number of the disciples multiplied greatly in Jerusalem, and a great many of the priests were obedient to the faith. (Acts 6:7)*
>
> *But the word of God grew and multiplied. (Acts 12:24)*
>
> *So the word of the Lord grew mightily and prevailed. (Acts 19:19,20)*

## APPLICATION

We are to model Jesus. Jesus has all authority. ***All authority in heaven and on earth has been given to Me ... going therefore ... teaching...*** (Matt. 28:18). Because of that truth, Jesus He gives the church that same authority and commands the church to go and ***make disciples***. They did ... ***daily teaching and preaching Christ*** (Acts 5:42). In John 1:14, the Scripture says that ***the Word became flesh***. In the Book of Acts the disciples went everywhere ***preaching the Word*** (Acts 4:31; 6:2,4; 8:4,25; 10:37,44; 15:7; 11:1,19; 12:24; 17:11; 19:20; et al). Why? Because He is Life. He is Truth. He is Power. The Word of God is the manifestation of Christ through the spoken word (II Pet. 2:19; II Tim. 4:2; I John 1:1; Rom. 1:15).

> *All Scripture is inspired of God and is profitable for doctrine, reproof ... (II Tim. 3:16)*
>
> *... study to show yourselves approved of God a workman that needs not to be ashamed, rightly dividing the Word of Truth. (II Tim. 3:15)*
>
> *... we preach Christ crucified ... (I Cor. 1:23)*

## **WE PREACH CHRIST, NOT AN IDEA OR DOCTRINE**

> *... they ceased not to teach and preach Jesus Christ ... (Acts 4:12; 5:42)*
>
> *... in Whom are hidden all the treasures of wisdom and knowledge. ... For in Him dwells all the fullness of the Godhead bodily; and you are complete in Him, who is the head of all principality and power. (Col. 2:3,9-10)*

We preach Christ. We teach doctrine. The Gospel is one of proclamation first. Jesus is the ***Light*** (John 8:12), **the *Way, the Truth, and the Life*** (14:6), ***the Resurrection and the Life*** (11:25), the ***Bread of Life*** (6:48), ***the Door*** (10:9), ***the Good Shepherd***[13] (10:11), and ***the True Vine*** (15:1). Make our message Christ-centered!

---

[13] I Cor. 1:30; Acts 17:3

*Jesus: The Model Missionary*

| PEOPLE ARE | CHRIST IS |
|---|---|
| To the Weak, | **Almighty God** |
| To the Sinner, | **Savior/Redeemer** |
| To the Sick, | **Jehovah-Rapha—Healer** |
| Need of Wisdom, | **Counselor** |
| Lonely, | **Lover of My Soul** |
| Hope, | **Resurrection and Life** |
| To the Lost, | **The Way, the Truth, and the Life** |
| To the Doubters, | **Author and Finisher of our Faith** |
| To the Unmarried, | **Bridegroom** |
| Representative, | **Our Advocate before God** |
| Blind, | **Blind Man Healed—spiritually gives sight** |
| Needing Guidance, | **Good, Great, and Chief Shepherd** |
| Struggling with Sin, | **He is our Sanctifier** |
| To Those in Prison to Sin/Self, | **He is the Jail-breaker** |
| To those in Darkness, | **He is the Light of the World** |
| To those who are Dead in Trespasses and Sin, | **Jesus is the Redeemer and Savior of the world!** |
| To those who are Hungry, | **He is the Bread of Life** |
| To those who are Weary, | **He said come unto Me and I will give you rest** |
| To those who are Thirsty, | **He says drink of Me and you will never thirst again** |
| To those who are Broken-hearted, | **He heals the Broken-hearted** |
| To those who are Dead in Trespasses and Sin, | **He says I am the Resurrection and the Life** |
| To those without a Father, | **He is the Everlasting Father** |
| To those Hell-bound, | **He is the Way, the Truth, and the Life to Heaven** |

## THE APOSTLES SAW THE NEED

- Repentance – Acts 2:18; 3:19; 8:22; 11:18
- Faith – Acts 2:44; 3:16; 4:4, 32; 6:5,7,8; 8:12; 13:37; 9:42; 10:43; 11:17,21 (a gift of God that must be appropriated), Acts 5:31; 11:18; Eph. 2:8

## LORDSHIP OF CHRIST[14]

What is a disciple? A disciple is a person who receives Jesus Christ as Savior, and follows Him as Lord of his or her life. A disciple follows Jesus Christ. It means to *take up the (His) Cross and follow Me*. It means sacrifice. The claims of Christ come first. Then a disciple's life finds true joy and peace with God. The church is not to win converts (souls) to a denomination or church membership, but to Christ ... to impart His nature, integrity and character. Not confined to Israel, but to all nations—the entire world. It is Christ's by right of creation (John 1:3) and redemption (John 3:17)—internationally, interracially, and intercultural. What does it mean to follow Christ and to make Him Lord of our lives?

### 1) VOLUNTARY

It is not pleasing to self. It is a denial of self and its selfish and personal ambitions. It is for the sake of Christ. We surrender our likes and desires to Him. It is our choice that we make to follow His call. We follow Him that He might receive glory. We get the benefits of Him Who loves us dearly and wants our very best.

### 2) CONTINUOUS (DAILY)

It is not just a one-time event. *Follow Me*, Jesus says—in joys, sorrow, on mountain tops, in valleys, even in persecution or martyrdom. I will be with you. *I will never to leave nor forsake you*, even in the valleys of your experience. That is My promise to you!

### 3) ABSOLUTELY NECESSARY FOR TRUE CONVERSION

Then, calling the crowd to join his disciples, he said,

> *If any of you wants to be my follower, you must turn from your selfish ways, take up your cross, and follow me. For whoever desires to save his*

---

[14] Luke 9:23,24; 14:27; Matt. 10:38,39; 16:24,25; Mark 8:34

*life will lose it, but whoever loses his life for My sake and the gospel's will save it. Or what will it profit a man if he gains the whole world, and loses his own soul? Or what will a man give in exchange for his soul? And he who does not take his cross and follow after Me is not worthy of Me. He who finds his life will lose it, and he who loses his life for My sake will find it. (Mark 8:34-39, NLT; see John 12:23-26)*

---

"Never try to choose the place of martyrdom."
—O. Chambers

---

## 4) NOT PLEASING SELF

To love Christ more than any other relationship is so supremely important it could compared to *hating* for some. No exceptions.

*Anyone who wants to be my follower must love me far more than he does his own father, mother, wife, children, brothers, or sisters—yes, more than his own life—otherwise he cannot be my disciple. And no one can be my disciple who does not carry his own cross and follow me. But don't begin until you count the cost. Otherwise, you might complete only the foundation before running out of money, and then everyone would laugh at you. They would say, 'There's the person who started that building and couldn't afford to finish it!' (Luke 14:26-30, NLT)*

*Whosoever does not bear his cross, and come after Me, cannot be my disciple. (Luke 14:27)*

When we make Christ our Lord, He is the sovereign Lord of our lives. He gives the loving orders. We obey, hopefully with joy! He gives us of Himself. His power, His peace, His protection, His love, His joy, His satisfaction, His provision ... His very Life become ours. He lives in us and we follow Him! Following Jesus is costly. ***Question:*** *Is it worth it? John 16:33 –* <u>*YES!!*</u>

## 5) SEPARATION

Jesus calls for separation with possessions that are possessing us (Matt. 19:21—rich young ruler; Luke 14:33). Sometimes it means a separation even from work, if necessary. The disciples left being a tax collector, fishermen, etc. (Mark 2:14).

> *Now it happened as they journeyed on the road, that someone said to Him, "Lord, will follow You wherever You go."*[15] *And Jesus said to him, "Foxes have holes and birds of the air have nests, but the Son of Man has nowhere to lay His head." Then He said to another, "Follow Me." But he said, "Lord, let me first go and bury my father." Jesus said to him, "Let the dead bury their own dead, but you go and preach the kingdom of God." And another also said, "Lord, I will follow You, but let me first go and bid them farewell who are at my house." But Jesus said to him, "No one, having put his hand to the plow, and looking back, is fit for the kingdom of God." (Luke 9:57-62; cf. Matt 8:18-22)*

## 6) IT IS FOR THE SAKE OF CHRIST

Christ calls us to be His disciple! You enter into My joys, My sorrows—on the mountains, in the valleys, and even in persecution and in martyrdom—all for My sake.

### **Rewards of Obedience and Testing of Faith**

> *"If you love Me, keep My commandments. And I will pray the Father, and He will give you another Helper, that He may abide with you forever. ... He who has My commandments and keeps them, it is he who loves Me. And he who loves Me will be loved by My Father, and I will love him and manifest Myself to him." ... Jesus answered and said to him, "If anyone loves Me, he will keep My word; and My Father will love him, and We will come to him and make Our home with him. He who does not love Me does not keep My words; and the word which you hear is not Mine but the Father who sent Me." (John 14:15-16,21,23-24)*

Faith will be tested in our walk with the Lord.

> *Therefore do not cast away your confidence, which has great reward. For you have need of endurance, so that after you have done the will of God, you may receive the promise. (Heb. 10:35-36)*

**Peter:** What reward shall we have in following you? You have been blessed. You have preached the Gospel, healed the sick, cast out devils. I have supplied all your needs, so that you lacked nothing. I have showered

---

[15] Matt. 19:29,30; James 1:2-5

you with so much grace. What are the rewards? We have been given eternal life to be with Christ forever. Believers will be sharing life as a family and receiving life of the Kingdom of God in the world to come (Luke 14:33; 18:28-30; Phil. 3:7-9 — Paul); Matt. 13:46 (pearl of great price). Our sins have been forgiven. What other reward shall be given us that are worth the price of following Christ?

> *Then Peter said to Him, "Behold, we have left everything and followed You; what then will there be for us?" And Jesus said to them, "Truly I say to you, that you who have followed Me, in the regeneration when the Son of Man will sit on His glorious throne, you also shall sit upon twelve thrones, judging the twelve tribes of Israel. And everyone who has left houses or brothers or sisters or father or mother or children or farms for My name's sake, will receive many times as much, and will Inherit eternal life. But many who are first will be last; and the last, first. (Matt 19:27-30 NASB)*

## **CONCLUDING NOTE**

Jesus was called and sent by the Father to both Jew and Gentile to fully identify with mankind (John 4:34; 17:8,18,25). He was sent to give His life a ransom. He came to serve and not be served. To follow Christ as our Missionary example we are to fully identify with people in their culture, yet without compromise. We are now the called and the sent ones—sent to preach, to heal, to cast out devils, and even to raise the dead. If those, to whom He has sent us, receive you, they receive Me. If they reject you, they reject Me (Luke 9:48; Matthew 10:16,40).

We are His ambassadors (II Cor. 5:20), invested with His power (Acts 1:8; 3:12-16), and authorized to use His Name (Acts 3:6; 4:10; John 14:12-14). We are to teach, to train up, and make students and followers of Christ—not only methods, but Christ Himself! (Luke 14:25-33).

# Chapter Eight

# Ministry

## INDIVIDUALS AS WELL AS GROUPS

Jesus gave us the model of what the Church is to be and what to do. The Church is to reach the whole world with the Gospel. Sinners were welcomed by Jesus. It is very important that we do not limit ourselves, unless God has called you to a particular people or area of society. To Him, ministering to an individual was as important as ministering to a multitude. He spoke to the religious leaders like Nicodemus (John 3) as well as speaking and healing the blind man, and speaking to sinners and hated tax collectors. He taught individuals and multitudes (Matt. 13:2; 15:30; 19:2; Luke 14:25). He healed individuals as well as fed the multitudes (Matt. 13:2; 15:30; 19:2; Luke 14:25). He taught individuals such as the rich young ruler (Luke 18:18-22) as well as the multitudes in the Sermon on the Mount. When He saw the city of Jerusalem and how they were rejecting Him, He wept. He saw the weeping of Mary and Martha and wept. He also wept at the death of Lazarus. He met with the woman of Samaria who then brought the whole city to see Jesus (John 4). He went to other cities, fulfilling the will of His Father (Luke 4:43). Much of the New Testament accounts record Jesus spending time with individuals. We cannot neglect the individuals when following Christ as our Model in mission. He went to every city and He was modeling to His disciples what He would command them to do.

> *Soon afterward Jesus began a tour of the nearby towns and villages, preaching and announcing the Good News about the Kingdom of God. He took his twelve disciples with him ... (Luke 8:1, NLT)*

Much of the New Testament records record Jesus having to do with individuals. The Holy Spirit is the Director of Missions, whether it is to a crowd or to one. The Church is to reach the whole world with the Gospel. It is very important that we do not limit ourselves, unless God has called you to a particular people or area of society.

## A. CROSS-CULTURAL—UNIVERSAL

The mission of the church is to the whole world, though some target certain groups for missions. The church is called to all classes, all peoples, to every nation.

> *For I am not ashamed of the gospel of Christ, for it is the power of God to salvation for everyone who believes, for the Jew first and also for the Greek. (Rom. 1:16)*

The disciples were sent first to the Jews—**to the lost sheep of the House of Israel** (Matt. 10:5,6). Later Jesus sent 70 others for the nations surrounding Israel, symbolizing the Gentile nations (Gen. 10). Some are sent to a particular people group.

He was also sent to the Gentiles (non-Jews). Jesus called them *other sheep* so that He would *gather all nations unto Him* (Matt. 25:32). He went to the Samaritan woman and the Samaritans (John 4:1-42). The disciples wanted to *"send fire"* on them. The disciples wanted to keep them out of the Kingdom (Luke 9:28,29,51-56). Jesus included them. Samaritans were considered **"dogs"** to the Jews—the unreachable, the undesirables. In India they are called the **"untouchables."** Who are the people that need to be reached with the Gospel? What specific group?

For those in countries long term, one should learn the culture, speak the language, be sensitive, sincere, adapt, and adopt where you can. God is not willing that any should perish—from every people group, from every nation, from every language (II Pet. 3:9; Acts 13:47).

## Illustration

Jesus brought healing to the demon-possessed daughter of a Canaanite woman from Tyre and Sidon (Greek; Matt. 15:21-28). He delivered a demoniac of the Gadarenes, a Roman province (Mark 5:1-20) and a servant was restored to a Roman centurion (Mark 8:5-13; Matt. 8:5-15). He healed a deaf man of Decapolis, a Greek-Roman city (Mark 7:31-37). It was Jesus who, in cleansing the temple, said, *My house shall be called a house of prayer for all nations* (Mark 11:17; Isa. 56:7). There is only one Church, one Flock, and one Shepherd.

The <u>Parable of the Weeds</u> (Matt. 13:34-30; 26-43) illustrates this truth. The field is the world. Christ is laying claim to all He has created.

*They will come from the east and the west, from the north and the south, and sit down in the kingdom of God. (Luke 13:29)*

*Assuredly, I say to you, wherever this gospel is preached in the whole world ... (Mark 14:9)*

In the book of John, the Godhead is universal in His redemption.

| Father | • God so loved the <u>world</u> (*kosmos*; John 3:16,17,19) |
|---|---|
| Son | • Lights every man that comes into the world (John 1:9)<br>• The Lamb of God who takes away the sins of the world (John 1:29)<br>• That this is indeed the Christ, the Savior of the world (John 4:42)<br>• For the bread of God is He who comes down from heaven and gives life to the world (John 6:33)<br>• Light of the world (John 8:12)<br>• I came not to judge the world, but to save the world (John 12:47) |
| Holy Spirit | • The Spirit convicts the world of sin, righteousness, and judgment (John 16:8) |

## **Illustration: Two Ocean Liners**

The story of two ocean liners illustrates for us the challenges of reaching the world for Christ. Both liners begin to sink with many people on board who do not know how to swim. There are ten rescuers in the two large rescue boats. In the first liner, hundreds are sinking, some holding on to debris. Several hundred yards away, the same is taking place with the other ocean liner. There are lots of room and help in a rescue boat. The cry for help comes from both ocean liners. Love cannot be the only motive for the rescue, for distant souls are the same as those that are near. To row to the other ship would deplete the energies of resources meaning less people saved. Love may refuse to leave the rescue of one to go to other. The issue is not to necessarily maximize the total number of individuals saved. The dilemma is faced by many on the mission field as well as pastors.

When Jesus spoke to the Samaritan woman, He left many who needed salvation. Why? He was doing the will of His Father, not counting heads as to the number of souls. Even the Samaritans who had heard the revelation of Jesus from this woman at the well, begged Him not to leave them (John 4:40). God's view is that there would be rescue operations for every people of the world, from both ocean liners, even if those who could rescue must leave a faithful "reached" people (first ocean liner) in order to labor among a possibly less fruitful "unreached people" (second ocean liner). Much of the New Testament records have to do with Jesus and many individuals.

Jesus left a successful ministry to go to **other cities** so that they too would be reached with the message of salvation (Luke 8:1; Mark 1:38,39; Luke 13:22). He went to Capernaum, Tyre and Sidon in Philistia, Decapolis; to a Syrophoenician (Greek), Samaritans, a Roman Centurion; to Caesarea, Philippi, Dalmatia, Gadara, Bethsaida, Nazareth, and Judea/Jordan. He went to a distant boat to rescue others.

## Application

God has made redemption available to all peoples, without exceptions. The challenge to the church is to preach the Gospel also to the unreached of our world. Today, those in missions estimate that 90% of missionaries work is done in 94% of already reached peoples of the world. The 10-40 window has the most unreached people in world. Jesus the Model Missionary asks us to Identify with the culture without loss of identity, to enter into other people's worlds, as Christ did with us. This can be done without compromising our Christian conviction, values, or standards. The Lord is not asking us to take away the culture or change it unless it violates Scripture. Examples of things we are not called to change are song, dress, mannerisms, family, etc. There is not a form or practice that is a requirement for entrance into the Christian community, except repentance and faith in Jesus Christ. We need to respect culture without compromising Biblical truth. The task of missions is not to reach as many people as possible, but to win individuals from all people groups of the world. Missiologists estimate that there are 6,854 people groups that have not heard the Gospel. That is still 41.6% of the world's population of 7 billion people. That is 2.87 billion people yet to hear the Gospel!

> *For "everyone who calls on the name of the Lord will be saved." But how can they call on him to save them unless they believe in him? And how can they believe in him if they have never heard about him? And*

*how can they hear about him unless someone tells them? And how will anyone go and tell them without being sent? That is why the Scriptures say, "How beautiful are the feet of messengers who bring good news!" (Rom. 10:13-15, NLT)*

## Illustration

Joe Gordon, a missionary to the people of the Himalayan mountains in north India climbed 10,000 feet with two others to speak to four families! It took them several days to climb and several days to return—all for four families! Was it worth it? Time? Effort? Expense? Yes! The Good Shepherd left the ninety and nine to rescue one lost sheep. One cannot place value on one soul in terms of time or expense. Jesus died for everyone individually. He died that these four families would become worshipers of Him. It was Jesus who left the crowd to talk to one Samaritan woman of low repute. Why? He was seeking a *worshiper.*

# CHAPTER NINE

# Teaching and Preaching in Word and Works

**KINGDOM OF GOD**[16]

The focal point of Christ's proclamation and most prominent in the teaching of Christ was the Kingdom of God. He began with it preaching (Mark 1:14,15) and ended with a discourse on it (Acts 1:3). The ***Kingdom*** is mentioned 60-plus times in the Gospels.

What is the Kingdom of God? The kingdom of God is the rule of an eternal sovereign God over all creatures and things. One enters into the Kingdom of God at the new birth; it is synonymous with the Kingdom of Heaven. Christ is King of the universe. It is His dominion. He has sovereign and absolute authority over the people that belong to that realm (Psa.103:1-9; 145:11,13). God established two priorities for mankind: the Kingdom of God and the righteousness of God (Matt. 6:25-34; 5:6). The word "Kingdom" is used 60 times in the Gospel records.

When shall Christ's Kingdom come (Matt. 24:3-14)? Jesus preached the Gospel of the Kingdom immediately following his baptism by John: ***The time is fulfilled, and the Kingdom of God has come near: repent and believe the Gospel*** (Mark 1:15). To truly believe the Gospel is to submit to another Authority in Christ. It is good news! Many of Jesus' parables taught the Kingdom of God and the Kingdom of Heaven. His Promise will be fulfilled—***This Gospel of the Kingdom shall be preached to the whole world as a witness to every nation [all people groups], and then shall the end come***

---

[16] Matt. 4:23 (teaching in their synagogues and preaching the Gospel of the Kingdom, and healing all manner of sickness and all manner of disease among the people; first message); Mark 1:14,15; Acts 1:3 (last message)

*(Matt. 24:14)*. After His resurrection, He spoke to His disciples concerning the Kingdom of God.

> ... *to whom He also presented Himself alive after His suffering by many infallible proofs, being seen by them during forty days and speaking of the things pertaining to the kingdom of God. (Acts 1:3—last message of Christ)*

The disciples had the physical kingdom in mind (Luke 19:11; Acts 1:4-6). Jesus had something else in mind. He was talking about the universal reign of God in the hearts of men and in the world (I Cor. 15:28; Rev. 11:15). **The Kingdom of God is the rule of the King in the inner man; the Kingdom is within you** (Luke 17:21). The Gospel is the Gospel of the Kingdom (Acts 4:23; 24:14; Acts 20:25; 28:23,31). It is the task of the Church to make the invisible Kingdom within visible to the world in word and deed. The parables illustrated to the disciples the truth of the Kingdom of God (see Matthew 13).

The Kingdom was ***not in word only but in power*** ... the power of God (Matt. 4:23; I Cor. 4:20). The Kingdom is the Lordship of Christ in absolute authority in the Church (Eph. 1:23; Col. 1:18). It is absolute ownership, for He is the Head of the Church. Repentance in submission to Christ is necessary to enter into the Kingdom of God (Matt. 3:2; 4:17; 12:28). The Kingdom of God was present when ***He cast out devils*** (Matt. 12:28; Luke 11:20). ***The Kingdom of God*** *has come near to you* when the disciples were told to heal the sick (Luke 10:9). It was that reality that Jesus gave to the disciples to carry on after He left this world.

## THE RULE OF GOD IN THE HEART OF MAN

> ... *for the kingdom of God is not eating and drinking, but righteousness and peace and joy in the Holy Spirit. (Rom. 14:17)*

> ... *nor will they say, "See here!" or "See there!" For indeed, the kingdom of God is within you. (Luke 17:21)* [17]

## RULED BY LOVE

> *Owe no one anything except to love one another, for he who loves another has fulfilled the law. ... "You shall love your neighbor as yourself."*

---

[17] Matt. 4:17; 7:21

> *Love does no harm to a neighbor; therefore love is the fulfillment of the law. (Rom. 13:8-10)*

Jesus taught how to **enter** into the Kingdom of God.

> *Unless one is born again, he cannot see the Kingdom of God. ... Most assuredly, I say to you, unless one is born of water and the Spirit, he cannot enter the kingdom of God. (John 3:3,5)*

> *For I say to you, that unless your righteousness exceeds the righteousness of the scribes and Pharisees, you will by no means enter the kingdom of heaven. (Matt. 5:20)*

## THE RULE OF GOD OVER HIS CHURCH

It is setting people free from demonic and ungodly infirmities (John 8:31,32; Acts 14:22 ... ***that we through much tribulation enter into the Kingdom of God;*** Acts 19:8; 20:25; 28:23,31). It was Paul's message while in a Roman prison preaching the Kingdom of God (Acts 19:8, 20:25; 28:23,31). To Him belongs all the rights, authority, and rulership in the Church. He bestows gifts. He is the sovereign Lord of the Church (Eph. 4:7,11; II Cor. 5:20). Christ is the Lord of the Church and the Church is His Body (Eph. 1:23; Rom.12:5; Col. 1:18).

> *And He put all things under His feet, and gave Him to be head over all things to the church, which is His body, the fullness of Him who fills all in all. (Eph. 1:22,23)*

> *And He is the head of the body, the church, who is the beginning, the firstborn from the dead, that in all things He may have the preeminence. (Col. 1:18)*

## THE RULE OF GOD IN THE WORLD

Christ will ultimately rule over the world and destroy the Kingdom of the devil (Rev. 12:10). Since He has the rule of all nations, His church will constitute believers from among all nations. God is the God of the nations.

> *Now when all things are made subject to Him, then the Son Himself will also be subject to Him who put all things under Him, that God may be all in all. (I Cor. 15:28)*

## LORDSHIP OF CHRIST[18]

*Therefore, God elevated him to the place of highest honor and gave him the name above all other names, that at the name of Jesus every knee should bow, in heaven and on earth and under the earth, and every tongue confess that Jesus Christ is Lord, to the glory of God the Father. (Phil. 2:9-11, NLT)*

*For John came unto you in the way of righteousness, and ye believed him not: but the publicans and the harlots believed him: and ye, when ye had seen it, repented not afterward, that ye might believe him. (Matt. 21:32, KJV)*

## SOME CHARACTERISTICS OF THE KINGDOM

- Matt. 20:25-28 – Leaders rule as servants, not lords.
- Matt. 5:11,12 – The citizens are meek, pure, peaceable, and forgiving.
- Eph. 1:23; Rom. 12:5; Col. 1:18 – It is the rule of Christ in the Church.
- Matt. 12:28 – It is the presence of Christ.
- Eph. 4:7-11; I Cor. 12-14; II Cor. 5:20 – The King, as Sovereign, appoints and bestows gifts.
- John 20:22; Matt. 16:17 – Christ gives authority to others.
- Rev. 5:13,14 – The King receives worship.
- I Cor. 3:13; Rev. 2,3 – He rewards and evaluates.
- Acts 14:22; 19:8; 20:25; 28:23,31 – It was the Kingdom that Paul preached.
- Matt. 13:31-46 – It is the Kingdom that is coming.

Evil will increase in the last days. There will be much deception to turn away people from Christ. There will be false religions and false enemies. There will be wars and rumors of wars, famines, earthquakes, persecution and martyrdom. Believers will be super-hated. Men will stumble and deliver up one another. There will be false prophets, sin shall increase, and the love of many shall wax cold (Matt. 25:4-12). However, God has not abandoned the world. Evil shall increase, and Satan, the god of this world, will continue to be hostile and cause the defeat of many. The Church will come under attack and many shall fall away. But, the Kingdom of God shall prevail—the Kingdom of God, through the Church, shall accomplish the ultimate purpose of God (Matt.

---

[18] Eph. 1:20-22; Rom. 13:8-10

25:14). The message is the Gospel of Christ. The motive is to make the way for the return of the King, Christ! The mission and goal of Christ is to establish a community of His Kingdom within every people group in the world which are capable of multiplying congregations into a fellowship of a local church.

## KINGDOMS IN CONFLICT

*We are at war!* When Jesus gave the Great Commission, it was a declaration of war. The battle is in the heavenlies—the conflict of the ages is the Kingdom of Light versus the kingdom of darkness— *the prince of the power of the air* (Eph. 2:2). Satan is called the *prince of this world* (John 12:31) and the *spirit that now works in the sons of disobedience* (Eph. 2:2).

Satan targets our faith (I Thess. 3:5). The word for *fight* in I Timothy 6:12 and I Peter 1:10 is used continually in describing the Christian life. *Strive* to enter into that rest (Heb.4:11; Luke 13:24; Rom. 15:30). Other words used for the battle include *struggling* (Col. 1:29). Paul defines his ministry as *not waging war according to the flesh* (II Cor. 10:3-5). We are to *wage a good warfare* (I Tim. 1:18), putting on *the whole armor of God* (Eph. 6:12-18). Missions and the ministry are warfare! The Kingdom of Light versus the kingdom of darkness. God's Kingdom shall prevail (Rev. 11:15)!

Christ, the King who is sovereign, appoints, and bestows gifts (Eph. 4:7-11; I Cor. 12-14), gives authority (John 20:22,23, Matt. 16:19), receives worship (Rev. 5:13,14), rewards and evaluates (Rev. 2,3), and is the Head of the Kingdom that is coming (Matt. 13:31-46). We are commissioned to preach the Kingdom of God *and teach those things which concern the Lord Jesus Christ* (Acts 8:12; 14:22; 19:8; 28:31). We represent Him as the King of kings and Lord of lords.

The Bible teaches that we are either in the *Kingdom of His dear Son* or in the *kingdom of darkness* (Col. 1:13). Preaching the Gospel, then, becomes the spiritual conflict of the ages where the power of God overthrows the *god of his world* who blinds the minds of the hearer and is the one who has had control over mankind (II Cor. 4:4). There is a power encounter with evil forces. Our Gospel is a Gospel of power—power to defeat the enemy of our souls ... power to change lives ... power to break habits of sin ... power to love ... power to forgive ... power to live holy lives ... power to witness of Christ ... power to give us new life in Jesus Christ. *Christ is the Power of God* (I Cor. 1:24)! His Kingdom shall prevail in victory. Jesus assured His disciples that at the end of life, He would share with them the blessings of the Kingdom (Luke 22:22-30). He promised that He would appear again to bring the blessedness of the Kingdom to those for whom it was prepared (Matt. 25:31,34). The struggle will continue until the Gospel is preached in all the world, and then the end shall come (Matt. 24:14).

> *And He said to them, I saw Satan fall like lightning from heaven. Behold, I give you the authority to trample on serpents and scorpions, and over all the power of the enemy, and nothing shall by any means hurt you. (Luke 10:18,19)*
>
> *But you are those who have continued with Me in My trials. And I bestow upon you a kingdom, just as My Father bestowed one upon Me ... (Luke 22:28,29)*

Our Lord's ministry and announcement and proclamation of the Good News of the Kingdom was characterized by healing, and most notably by the casting out of demons in delivering men from the bondage of Satan (Matt. 12:28). What is the explanation of Jesus' power? He cast out evil spirits *by the Spirit of God* (Matt. 12:28). He preached *the Gospel of the Kingdom* ... with the Spirit of God (Matt 6:33; Mark 1:14,15; Luke 4:43). It is the Good News of God's rule in the hearts and lives of those who submit by faith to His Lordship.

The King who is sovereign Ruler of the universe appoints and bestows gifts (Eph. 4:7-11; I Cor. 12-14), gives **authority** (John 20:22,23; Matt. 16:19, **receives worship** (Rev. 5:13,14), **rewards and evaluates** (Rev. 2,3), and it is **His Kingdom that is coming** (Matt. 13:31-46). We represent Him (Matt. 10:40; II Cor. 5:20). We are **commissioned to preach** the Kingdom of God *and teach those things which concern the Lord Jesus Christ* (Acts 8:12; 14:22; 19:8; 28:31). The life which Christ came to bring us is the life of God's Kingdom.

## CHRIST'S KINGDOM TRIUMPHS – THE FINAL VICTORY ASSURED

### 1) <u>Victory over Death</u>[19]

The Gospel of the Kingdom is an announcement of Christ's conquest over death. Satan had power over death because the *sting of death is sin* but Jesus came to *destroy him who had the power of death, that is, the devil* (Heb. 2:14,15). On the Cross, the last enemy of death for every man in life was

---

[19] John 5:24; 8:51,52; I Cor. 15:24-26 —— the "last enemy" is death

conquered. That is the Good News—the death, resurrection, and ascension of Christ, as well as the Second Coming! That is the Gospel: the perfect blessings of God's reign (John 11:25,26; 5:21; 6:35,39,40; John 1:4; I John 1:1,2; 5:11).

> *O death, where is thy sting? O grave, where is thy victory? The sting of death is sin; and the strength of sin is the law. But thanks be to God, which gives us the victory through our Lord Jesus Christ. Therefore, my beloved brethren, be ye steadfast, unmovable, always abounding in the work of the Lord, forasmuch as ye know that your labor is not in vain in the Lord. (I Cor. 15:55-58)*

Christ is our hope (I Tim. 1:1). The world does not have hope (Eph. 2;12; I Thess. 4:13). It is **Christ in you, the HOPE of Glory** (Col. 1:27).

2) <u>Victory over Satan</u>

He is called the ***prince of this world*** (Luke 14:3; Matt. 23:29; Luke 10:18).

> *Now is the judgment of this world; now the ruler of this world will be cast out. (John 12:31)*

> *Or how can one enter a strong man's house and plunder his goods, unless he first binds the strong man? And then he will plunder his house. (Matt. 12:29)*

In I Pet. 5:8, Satan is described as a ***roaring lion***. He still roars, but he has been defeated. Satan has a kingdom also. He has principalities and powers. He tempts us to doubt and to fear. He tempts us to sin. He is a thief, a liar, a deceiver, and a murderer. He is called a dragon, an adversary, and an accuser of the brethren. Thank God for Christ Who is the Victor. He won the victory on the Cross, and in the Resurrection and His Ascension.

> *In this way, he disarmed the spiritual rulers and authorities. He shamed them publicly by His victory over them on the cross. (Col. 2:15, NLT)*

> *But when people keep on sinning, it shows they belong to the devil, who has been sinning since the beginning. But the Son of God came to destroy these works of the devil. (I John 3:8, NLT)*

Jesus in the flesh won the victory where Adam failed. Jesus came *to* **destroy the works of the devil** (I John 3:8). The Bible says that we were **following the prince of the power of the air** (Eph. 2:2). We are no longer under Satan's kingdom. We have been set free by the power of the Gospel and we are now in the Kingdom of Jesus Christ. We now have hope. Our guarantee is in Christ! ***HALLELUJAH!!***

### 3) Victory over Sin

**Jesus is the Victor**...the **Conqueror** over all sin, not only in the forgiveness of sin, but in its power to control us. ***Whosoever commits sin is a servant to sin ... whom the Son sets free is free indeed*** (John 8:34-36). There is hope for those plagued by repeated failures. He loves you and wants you to be free. His grace and His power are available to free you, to deliver you from the snare and traps that Satan and the flesh have made for you.

There may be those reading this who are struggling with sin, with habits that you cannot leave. Some of you have tried in your own strength to have the victory over pornography or other sins of the mind or flesh. Some of you may have been flirting with sin. You have opened the door, maybe to sexual temptation or some other sin that could destroy you.

The Bible says that we have been ***crucified with Christ*** and we have also been ***raised together with Christ*** (Rom. 6:6). Christ has abolished Satan, death, and sin (Heb. 9:26). The power of sin has been broken. In Christ's Kingdom there is freedom, hope, and a guarantee of victory. **Jesus is the Victor**. He loves you and wants you to be free. His grace and His power are available to free you—to deliver you from the snare and traps that Satan and the flesh have made for you. Today is another day in your life. Jesus makes a way of escape. The Bible says that we ***have been crucified with Christ*** and we have been ***raised together with Christ*** (Rom. 6:6). Christ has abolished Satan, death, and sin (Heb. 9:26). Call upon the Lord, turn from your sin, and obey His Word and Spirit for daily victory.

> *No temptation has overtaken you except such as is common to man; but God is faithful, who will not allow you to be tempted beyond what you are able, but with the temptation will also make the way of escape, that you may be able to bear it. (I Cor. 10:13)*

## **THE KINGDOM OF GOD AND MIRACLES**

The Gospel of the Kingdom was not only for salvation, but included miracles.

> *And heal the sick there, and say to them, "The kingdom of God has come near to you." (Luke 10:9)*

> *And Jesus went about all Galilee, teaching in their synagogues, preaching the gospel of the kingdom, and healing all kinds of sickness and all kinds of disease among the people. (Matt. 4:23)*

Throughout the ministry of Jesus there were always miracles. That is the ministry He gave to His disciples and to His church today. These were an integral in preaching the Kingdom of God.

> *And heal the sick there, and say to them, the kingdom of God has come near to you. (Luke 10:9)*

> *These signs shall follow them that believe ... they shall cast out demons, and they shall lay hands on the sick and they shall recover. (Mark 16:17,18)*

That promise is still true today. Many thousands of miracles are taking place regularly around the world, with even some testimonies of people being raised from the dead.

## WHAT IS THE PURPOSE OF MIRACLES?

### A. For the Glory of God

> *This sickness is not unto death, but for the glory of God, that the Son of God may be glorified through it. (John 11:4; 2:11; 9:3)*

> *One Sabbath day as Jesus was teaching in a synagogue, he saw a woman who had been crippled by an evil spirit. She had been bent double for eighteen years and was unable to stand up straight. When Jesus saw her, he called her over and said, "Dear woman, you are healed of your sickness!" Then he touched her, and instantly she could stand straight. How she praised God! (Luke 13:10-13, NLT)*

> *So the crowd marveled as they saw the mute speaking, the crippled restored, and the lame walking, and the blind seeing; and they glorified the God of Israel. (Matt. 15:31; 9:8)*

### B. To Witness and to Confirm the Gospel

He said My works demonstrate who I am (John 10:24,25; John 20:31; 21:25; Rom. 15:18,19); ***the works that I do in My Father's Name, they bear witness of Me*** (John 5:36); ***the Father does the works*** (John 14:10,11); Matthew 12:10

(man with withered hand – witness of who He was); Matthew 8:28-34 (wild man of the Gadarenes –the whole city came out to meet Jesus). Miracles inspire faith. What I see in others can happen to me. The miracle of the water turned to wine was *to* **manifest His glory** (John 2:11); ***and when they had seen the things that Jesus did, believed on Him*** (John 11:45,47,48; *Matt. 8:24-28; John 6:14; 11:45,47)*

> *The very works that I do by the power of My Father bear witness concerning Me ... they are My credentials and evidence in support of Me. (John 10:25)*

Not all people will believe, even though they see miracles. Some will still doubt because their heart is hardened **even if raised from the dead** *(Luke 16:31)*, while some will experience miracles from the devil, at times (Acts 8:9-25 – Simon).

> *And truly Jesus did many other signs in the presence of His disciples, which are not written in this book; but these are written that you may believe that Jesus is the Christ, the Son of God, and that believing you may have life in His name. (John 20:30,31)*

> *But I have a greater witness than John's; for the works which the Father has given Me to finish—the very works that I do—bear witness of Me, that the Father has sent Me. (John 5:36)*

> *Paul, through mighty signs and wonders by the power of the Spirit of God ... (Rom. 15:18,19)*

## C. Growth of Church (Book of Acts) [20]

> *Then they that gladly received his word were baptized: and the same day there were added unto them about three thousand souls. (Acts 2:41)*

> *... and they were filled with wonder ... and many who heard the word believed and the number of the men was about 5,000. (Acts 3:10; 4:4)*

> *... they scattered everywhere preaching the Gospel ... with signs and wonders. (Acts 8:4; cf. Mark.16:15)*

---

[20] Acts 2:47; 5:12,14; 6:7; 9:33-42; John 11:45

## D. His Works Authenticate His Messianic Claim

*Then the Jews surrounded Him and said to Him, "How long do You keep us in doubt? If You are the Christ, tell us plainly." Jesus answered them, "I told you, and you do not believe. The works that I do in My Father's name, they bear witness of Me." (John 10:24,25)*

## E. His works were also to alleviate human suffering.

*... who went about doing good ... teaching, preaching and healing all that were oppressed by the devil. (Acts 10:38; cf. Matt. 4:23; 11:2-6)*

## APPLICATION

We need to see more of the miraculous—more of the supernatural in our life and in the ministry. Though many of us may not have the gift of healing, there is still power and authority in the Name of Jesus ... in ***My NAME*** (Mark 16:15,16). It is the same today as it was in Jesus' day. They came to see and experience the miracle. Miracles still attract people to Christ and the greatest attraction to the church today!

# Chapter Ten

# Training of the Twelve

Jesus came not only to redeem the world. He also came to train those who would be followers of Him when He would depart. He came to disciple His followers, something He commands us to do in the Great Commission. Although Jesus was only 30 years of age when He began His public ministry for three years, we know His calling and personal discipleship of His disciples was profound (Matt. 20:17; Mark 6:31). Jesus always had His departure in focus (Mark 8:31; John 7:33; 13:1; 16:17; Mark 2:20).

One of the ways He prepared to ascend back to His Father was to reproduce Himself in His disciples. He focused on the training of the twelve. He never lost sight of His goal of redemption, but men were His method—not programs—to reach the multitudes. He took them aside. They were to be His witnesses of His Person, His doctrine, His manner of life, His patience, and His teaching. They were changed by His presence. He gathered His disciples before He organized an evangelistic campaign or even preached a public sermon (Matt. 4:19; Mark 3:14). He recognized that the building of His Church and the prevailing of His Kingdom begins with individuals, not groups; persons not programs—spirit, not matter. He appointed them to preach, to heal, and to cast out devils, and even **raise the dead** (Matt. 10:8)!

He taught them in word and in deed. He taught them by example to *take up your Cross and follow Me* (Matt. 16:25). He taught that to **lose one's life** is to gain life (Mark 8:34-38). His life in teaching, preaching, and ministry became a model of their own, as the Book of Acts demonstrates. He encouraged them (Matt. 16:17,19). They were accountable to Him (Mark 6:30; Luke 9:10). He taught them faith (Mark 4:35-41). He trusted them to be further molded by God (Luke 22:32; John 14:12). They participated in ministry with Him (Mark 5:37-44; 8:1-9,27). He said, *where I am, there will My servant be also* (John 12:26). He never gave up on them, even with their unbelief (Matt. 17:20; Luke 9:40,41) and doubt (Matt. 14:31). He corrected them (Mark 8:14-21,33; 9:17-19), rebuked them for their hardness of heart (Matt. 16:14), and for their internal wrangling for personal position (Matt. 20:20; Mark 10:35; Luke 22:24), and gave personal instruction (Mark 8:17). He was denied by Peter and abandoned by all (Matt. 12:35; 26:56). But Jesus never gave up on them. However, it was Peter who preached the first message at Pentecost, having denied the Lord 10 days earlier, and the disciples became the foundation of the Early Church. Oh, what grace! Jesus promised that His Kingdom should prevail in spite of persecution and martyrdom (Matt. 6:18).

Jesus modeled what He commands us to do in the Great Commission. This is different from evangelism which is an outreach to the lost, sometimes a one-time event, a witness on the street or in the workplace. This should be one of the main emphases of a pastor, to disciple those the Lord has placed under his tutorship! In the long term, Jesus is building His Church, a fellowship of the redeemed who will be His Voice and reincarnation in a city, country, and the world. Reproduced to reproduce, like a grain of mustard seed that becomes greater than all herbs (Matt. 13:32; cf. Mark 4:32; Luke 13:18,19). The disciples were first-hand witnesses of His doctrine, manner of life, patience, and teaching. There were changed by His presence. They were in turn to reproduce others through Christ. He not only ***commissioned*** them (Luke 10:1), but ***empowered*** them (Matt. 10:1; 28:18,19; Acts 1:8).

Jesus in preparing for His departure gave His disciples the right to use His Name and authority in future ministry (John 14:12-14; 16:23,24,26). His training on earth was complete as He sent His disciples and those who would follow, baptizing them in the Holy Spirit, and sending them into the world to make other disciples. The cycle would be complete (II Tim. 2:2).

> *Then He appointed twelve, that they might be with Him and that He might send them out to preach. (Mark 3:14)*

We are to follow Jesus as our Model Missionary. We are to model what we teach in word and deed. It goes back to the Great Commission to ***make disciples***. Lead by example and, as much as you can, take a small group of men, if possible, and disciple them. Do it over and over again with a new group of men. It may be somewhat difficult on the mission field or in a larger congregation. But if one can, spend time in the Word and in prayer, with discussion and joint participation in ministry, even with a few. Give yourself to them. Pour out of your life in serving them. Multiply yourself through these men. Challenge them in Bible reading and memorization, if possible writing down their thoughts during this special time with them, and send them on projects or go with them in missions projects and ministry for "on the job training." Help them in discovering and releasing their gifts. Lead them by example as you build disciples and follow Jesus the Model Missionary! He took a few men while He ministered to the multitudes. He took three up to the Mount of Transfiguration. Reproduce yourselves; don't just evangelize. You do not know how long you have. Always see yourself as temporary. You are not here to impress the crowds but join with Christ in building His Church as a co-laborer (I Cor. 3:9,10). Paul followed the pattern of Christ in making disciples.

> *And the things that you have heard from me among many witnesses, commit these to faithful men who will be able to teach others also. (II Tim. 2:2)*

# Chapter Eleven

# Satanic Opposition

When Jesus gave the Great Commission, it was a declaration of war. The Kingdom of Light versus the Kingdom of Darkness. It is clearly seen in at least four places in the Book of Acts (chapters 8, 13, 16, 19). The power struggle will continue until the end of time.

*And this gospel of the kingdom will be preached in all the world as a witness to all the nations, and then the end will come. (Matthew 24:14)*

## WE ARE AT WAR

The first Adam was tempted (we do not know how long after he received the command from God not to eat of the fruit of the garden) and chose to disobey. He was judged in that he died. The Second Adam was tempted and chose to obey His Father and give life to all (Rom. 5:12-19). Each one of us has been tempted in one of these ways. We will all be tempted and tested in three areas of our lives.

Jesus was baptized in water, anointed with the Spirit, and was immediately driven by the Spirit into the wilderness to be tempted of the devil (Matt. 4:1-11; Mark 1:12; Luke 4:1-11).

> *Immediately [following water baptism and the descending of the Holy Spirit on Christ] the Spirit drove Him into the wilderness. And He was there in the wilderness forty days, tempted by Satan, and was with the wild beasts; and the angels ministered to Him. (Mark 1:12,13)*

## TEMPTATION[21]

Jesus' ***first*** temptation (**lust of the flesh** — *to turn stones to bread*) was to use His divine power to satisfy His own physical needs. Satan was saying, **Does**

---

[21] Matthew 4:1-11; Mark 1:12; Luke 4:12

**God really care?** If He does, why are You where You are now in your situation? Some of us might ask the same question of God, especially when in ministry. Why the opposition, why sickness, separation, attacks? If God really cared for me, why am I going through what I am going through? You should not be living in the conditions you are in. Turn the stones to bread. Satisfy your desires. Take the situation into you own hands. God has left you to go it alone.

Satan used the same temptation with Eve: 1) *Has God said* (**doubt the Word**); 2) You *shall not touch it* (**added to the Word**); 3) You *shall not die* (**denied the Word**). The argument is that God has given us desires and we have a right to satisfy them, even in ministry. The anointing is to obey God and His Word or to satisfy selfish or fleshly desires.

Jesus' response: *It is written!* It is not how I feel, not the opinion of others, not about the situation. The Word of God was His defense and offense! Our situation may change, but God's eternal Word does not change. It is eternal and the Voice of God. There was no argument of rationalism or defense. This is the first recorded word that Jesus spoke after He entered into the world. The challenge is to base our relationship on what happens to us rather than who we are in Christ.

> *But He answered and said, "It is written, 'Man shall not live by bread alone, but by every word that proceeds from the mouth of God.'" (Matt. 4:4; cf. Deut. 8:3)*

## ILLUSTRATION

The Israelites were not satisfied with Manna. They wanted quail to satisfy the flesh. (Ex. 16:3; Psa. 78:18; Num. 11:4-6)

The *second* temptation was the *lust of the eyes*. The temptation was to jump off the Temple and perform a spectacular feat so the people would follow Him, even if it was contrary to the Word of God. **Can you trust God?** Prove that you are the Son of God. Do something to tempt God to see if He will provide for you. Get your rewards now. You do not have to wait. Cast yourself down. Step out in faith and trust God, Satan might say to us. See if God will deliver you. Test Him to see if you really are a child of God. Surely, He would not allow any of His own to suffer! If you were in an emergency, could He be trusted to care for you? Take a risk. Get as close to danger and temptation as you can to see if God will spare you. God says that He would supply all needs. Get your rewards now. You do not have to wait. Cast yourself down. Test God to see if He and His promises are true. If you really are the Son of God, step out in faith and His angels will keep you.

Partial use of Scripture of a Scripture out of context to prove a point is unscriptural and dangerous! It is the same temptation he used with Eve at the Garden. Satan challenges or questions the Scriptures—**Has God said?** Satan tells you that one can compromise truth. I will take care of you in going beyond legitimate ministry needs and using carnal means to satisfy those needs. Covetousness in ministry is a challenge. I deserve more. I will do what it takes to get more, even if it means compromising truth to gain it.

> *Jesus said to him, "It is written again, 'You shall not tempt the LORD your God.'" (Matt. 4:7)*

The ***third*** temptation was ***the pride of life***. Satan says to Jesus: You can have the kingdom now, promised by Your Father, if you will bow down and worship me instead of your Father. The third temptation was to gain possession of the world by worshiping Satan. There is no need to wait for the future. You do not need to go to the Cross.

Satan's temptation is always out to divert us from God's way. Kingdom now! Pleasure now. Rewards now—riches, fame, position … all with some compromise. You can build the church through human efforts in your own power and abilities. You can do it, Satan says. Just compromise a little and worship me just a little and I will give you the kingdom now. Satan's temptation is always out to divert us from God's way. ***Just this once!*** Again, Jesus quoted the Scripture.

> *Then Jesus said to him, "Away with you, Satan! For it is written, 'You shall worship the LORD your God, and Him only you shall serve.'" (Matt 4:10)*

What motive lay behind all these temptations? Satan wanted to destroy Jesus' mission. Because Jesus' death would destroy Satan's power, Satan wanted Jesus to pollute His life and ministry. The ultimate issue behind these temptations was idolatry. The real purpose of Satan's temptation was that he might be worshiped instead of God. Bow down and worship me, just this once, and then do whatever you want. No one will know, except you and me. You are in the wilderness. Are you at that place in your life? You are tempted to compromise without anyone knowing that you did? Satan wants to take you away from Christ, His call on your life, and the reason for your being.

Satan tempted Eve the same way. 1) Doubt the Word: "***Hath God said***,"? 2) He denied the Word: "***You shall not surely die!***" 3) Satan added to the Word of God: *"neither shall you touch it, lest you die"* was not given by God (Gen. 3:1,3,4).

Jesus returned in the power of the Spirit—victoriously (Luke 4:14,18,19). He knows what it is to be tempted, like us, yet without sin. He gives us the same power of the Spirit to live victoriously.

> *So then, since we have a great High Priest who has entered heaven, Jesus the Son of God, let us hold firmly to what we believe. This High Priest of ours understands our weaknesses, for he faced all of the same testings we do, yet he did not sin. So let us come boldly to the throne of our gracious God. There we will receive his mercy, and we will find grace to help us when we need it most. (Heb. 4:14-16, NLT)*

## ILLUSTRATION

During the time of Caesar, an idol was set up for everyone to give allegiance to Caesar. All one had to do was take a pinch of salt and say, "Caesar is Lord." You did not have to scream it out, but just say it, and then do anything you pleased. No one would know. Just once ... even quietly. Those who did would not be martyred. They could live as they wanted, if they would just acknowledge Caesar!

Satanic opposition began before time when Satan declared his rebellion and treason against God (Isa. 14:13,14). Since he was cast down to earth, two kingdoms have existed side by side—the kingdom of Satan and the Kingdom of God. In Genesis 3:15, it was prophesied that Satan would bruise the heel of the woman (Christ). It was also prophesied that the same Seed (Christ) would crush Satan's head in final victory.

There is victory in the Word and in the Power of the Spirit to overcome the temptations (Rom. 8:31-37; Jude 9). We need to recognize the enemy (II Cor. 2:11). We are not ignorant of his devices to destroy us. He comes in many different forms. Sometimes as a ***roaring lion***, or an ***angel of light***, which is far more deceptive and dangerous.

In the Parable of the Sower, Christ is the King who is seeking to establish His Kingdom. He sows the seed with different results. Some fell on the ground, but the cares of this world, the deceitfulness of riches, and the lust for other things choked out the Word. Too busy. Too covetous of things. Christ mentions the birds of the air. The enemy sowed tares (weeds resembling wheat). The enemy of our souls knows how to slow us down—to get us to compromise truth, righteousness, and holy living. He tempts us with sex, money, position, or title. He gets our attention away from Christ to things of self and the flesh. We begin to cool off and die! (Matt. 13:18-23; Mark 4:14; Luke 8:11)

## ILLUSTRATION

In some of the Greek games, there were foot races. There was much competition with attempts to take advantage of one another. One strategy was to place women along the route of the runners, beautiful to make themselves available to delay the athlete to satisfy youthful lusts.

Another method was to roll in front of the runner a ball of solid gold. These balls of gold weighed the equivalent of one year's salary. Sometimes it would cause the runner to stoop down and pick up the "weight" thinking he could still run at the same pace. Gradually, however, this weight would take away the runner's energy, giving his opponent the advantage, causing the other runner to win. The enemy knows how to slow us down and get us distracted with sex, money, power, or position.

## THE QUESTION

Whom will you worship? In following Jesus our Model, we will be tempted! Satan says he has a lot to offer—the kingdoms of this world and their glory. Pleasure? Position? Power? You can have it now. No need to wait for the future. No need to go to the Cross. No need to sacrifice. Satan's temptation is always out to divert us from God's way. Once we compromise once, then it becomes easier to compromise again ... and again ... and again. And we are bound by the Satanic lies and deception.

We have many Old Testament examples of Satanic opposition. Nehemiah is a classic example. Sanballat and Tobiah tried to divert the building of the wall. They began to mock him and the workers, and offered a compromise to meet together. They made false accusations, temptations to sin, bombarded them with false prophets and the use of treachery. In every instance, Nehemiah and the people went to prayer. They overcame the insistent attacks of their enemies.

## SOME CONCLUSIONS

What are our temptations in the ministry? There are only three—the **lust of the flesh, the lust of the eyes, and the pride of life** (I John 2:16).

> *Do not love this world nor the things it offers you, for when you love the world, you do not have the love of the Father in you. For the world offers only a craving for physical pleasure, a craving for everything we see, and pride in our achievements and possessions. These are not from the Father, but are from this world. And this world is fading away, along with everything that people crave. But anyone who does what pleases God will live forever. (I John 2:15-17, NLT)*

## PURITY

There is always the challenge to purity—holiness of mind, spirit, and body. As a messenger of Christ, Satan will always confront us with temptation many times to compromise our relationship and commitment to Christ by yielding to temptation. Jesus knows what we are going through. He was **tempted in all points like as we are yet without sin.** He knows what it means to be tempted in the lust of the flesh, the lust of the eyes (covetousness), and the pride of life. The Lord promises to give us the victory over all temptations as we submit ourselves to Jesus as Lord of our lives, resist the devil, flee youthful lusts, guard ourselves (Jude 24), and follow after righteousness (II Tim. 3:22). He will keep us from falling.

Today, there are special challenges when it comes to the Internet. There are many pornography sites that are available. In the United States, there is a high percentage of pastors who are involved with pornography and a higher percentage of people in Church. It is crushing! It will destroy you if you open the door just a little. There is a strong temptation to open it just a little more … and more … and then you become sucked into the temptation of Satan to satisfy the lust of the flesh and the spirit of iniquity. You become a slave! Turn from it! Run from it! Get help, if need be. Call upon the Lord for deliverance.

In America, it is said that hundreds of ministers each month are failing. The primary reason is sexual uncleanness of some type. Some tell us that there are 25 million websites devoted exclusively to pornography. Promise Keepers, a men's organization in America, says that 65% of men struggle with some form of sexual addiction. Americans spend $57 billion a year on pornography, $20 million on child pornography alone!

## ATTACKS

Then there were the **physical** attacks of Satan. In Luke 4:28,29 the people of the town, filled with hatred, led Jesus to the edge of the hill to cast Him down. ***They took up stones to cast at Him, but Jesus hid himself*** (John

8:59). ***Again they sought to arrest him, but he escaped from their hands*** (John 10:39, ESV). Missionaries and pastors can verify such attacks in their ministry. Satan also tried to kill Jesus. In Luke 8:22-24, Jesus ***rebuked the wind.*** It was a Satanic attack to destroy Him physically.

## POSITION

Then there were the attacks on His **position**. The people said they would make Him king, before His time (John 6:15). You need not go to the Cross. Keep your life. No need to give it away. A waste! Satan would tell us the same. You are sacrificing too much. You can have what you desire now with a lot less sacrifice. Do any of you know the attacks of Satan like any of these? There were lies and accusations from religious leaders. ***Is it lawful to give taxes to Caesar? Show me a coin … Give to Caesar what is Caesar's and to God what is God's (Matt. 22:17-22).***

## THEOLOGY

There were attacks to challenge His **theological** position. The Sadducees challenged him on the issue of the Resurrection (Matt. 22:21). Spies were sent to entrap Him in His words (Luke 20:20). He was even accused of being demon possessed (Mark 3:20,21; Matt. 9:34; John 7:20).

> *Then the multitude came together again, so that they could not so much as eat bread. But when His own people heard about this, they went out to lay hold of Him, for they said, "He is out of His mind." (Mark 3:20,21, NLT)*

## FAMILY

The members of your family are asking for You. Who is My family? … Whoever does the things God wills is My brother, My sister, and My mother (Mark 3:32).

## SATANIC RULE

- John 12:31 (cast out); 14:30; 16:11 – the prince of this world is judged and has nothing in Me.
- II Cor. 4:4 – the god of this world has blinded the minds of them who believe not.
- I John 5:19 – the whole world lies under the power of the evil one.

- Eph. 2:2 – the ruler of the power of the air.
- Matt. 13:19,39 – the wicked one snatches away that which was sown in the heart.
- John 13:2,27 – the devil having put into the heart of Judas.
- Luke 22:3 – Satan entered into Judas (demon possession).

## NOTE

We are at war (Eph. 6:10-18; II Cor. 10:4-6). Ananias, **Why has Satan filled your heart to lie to the Holy Spirit?** (Acts 5:3). It occurred each time the Church penetrated further into enemy territory—Peter and John and Simon the sorcerer (Acts 8:14-23). In Acts 8:20-23, Simon Magus offered Peter money as a bribe. See also Acts 13:10 (Elymas, the sorcerer); 16:17 (baptism of Lydia – damsel possessed with the spirit of divination); 19:13-17 (seven sons of Sceva – tried to cast out devils *in the name of Jesus whom Paul preaches.*) Paul was at Ephesus with itinerate Jewish exorcists trying to duplicate the miracles and was attacked by a demon-possessed man (Acts 19:23-40). Anytime you will pursue God in a new dimension, spiritual warfare takes place. We are at war! We will encounter opposition.

## BATTLEGROUND

1. Mind – II Cor. 10:4,5; I Peter 2:11
2. Body – I John 2:16 (lust of the flesh); Gal. 6:16; Rom. 8:5; 13:14
3. Covetousness (lust of the eyes) – Gen. 3:6; Luke 4:5; Matt. 4:8; 5:28; Ecc. 5:10,11
4. Power (pride of life) – James 4:6; Luke 14:11; 18:14; Daniel 4:30; Prov. 21:14; Mark 7:21,22

---

Christ's Kingdom Triumphs – The Final Victory Is Assured!
Rev. 11:15

---

## EARLY CHURCH EXPERIENCED OPPOSITION

- Paul's message to open their eyes that they may turn from Satan (Acts 26:18).
- Paul in Samaria; Simon Magus— give me this power. Paul's response, repent ... you have no part in what is going on (Acts 8:20-23).

- Paul's First Missionary Journey; Elymas, the sorcerer, magician (Acts 16:17).
- Paul in Ephesus—center of worship of great goddess (Acts 19:15).
- II Cor. 4:4 – Satan has blinded their minds ...
- II Cor. 11 – false prophets – angels of light ... if an angel of light preach any other gospel, let him be accursed! (Gal. 1:8)
- II Cor. 2:11 – Satan takes advantage with legalism – not gospel of grace
- Matt. 13 – Parable of Sower – then comes the wicked one ... his enemy came and sowed ... the tares are the children of the wicked one ... the enemy that sowed them (tares) is the devil ... the Son of Man shall gather out of His Kingdom those things that offend ... and shall cast them into a furnace of fire.
- Eph. 2:2 – ... *you were following the paths of the prince of the power of the air.*
- I John 5:19 – *the whole world lies in the wicked one.*
- Eph. 4:27 – ... *neither give place to the devil ...*
- Acts 5:3 – *Why has Satan filled your heart to lie to the Holy Spirit?* (Ananias)

The same is true today, especially for those in ministry. Satan would tempt us to **the lust of the flesh** (lust, pornography, flirting, movies, television, I deserve a better wife/husband, etc.), **the lust of the eyes** of covetousness (I want more, I am not making enough money, greed, I am worth more; therefore, I will compromise truth for the sake of having more, greedy and materialistic, compromising integrity without regards to God's promise to provide all that we need), and **the pride of life** (the need for power, control, and authority beyond what God has given you, doing things my way, and not regarding others. I am the most important among our pastors, leaders, or workers. This is not a team effort, but a one-man show of power and the pride of life!)

We must guard ourselves. In Proverbs 1:7, it says, **the fear of the Lord is the beginning of wisdom.** *Again, ... the fear of the Lord is to hate evil* (Prov. 8:13, KJV). It is the love for our Heavenly Father, and having an understanding of who He is and what He represents that is the greater guard against temptation. His nature, His character, His holiness, and the knowledge that when we sin, we break the heart of God is the greatest deterrent. In Isaiah 52:11, it says to the priests that were handling the holy vessels in the Tabernacle to **be clean, you who bear the vessels of the Lord.** It is what Paul charged Timothy—to *flee youthful lusts, but follow righteousness* (II Tim. 2:21,22).

It is what Joseph did when he was tempted to sin with Potiphar's wife. He fled. He did not discuss it. He ran and feared the consequences from God greater than the consequences of the wrath of Potiphar's wife.

> *Therefore, come out from them and separate yourselves from them, says the Lord. Don't touch their filthy things, and I will welcome you.* (II Cor. 6:17, NLT)

> *You have heard that it was said to those of old, "You shall not commit adultery." But I say to you that whoever looks at a woman to lust for her has already committed adultery with her in his heart. If your right eye causes you to sin, pluck it out and cast it from you; for it is more profitable for you that one of your members perish, than for your whole body to be cast into hell. And if your right hand causes you to sin, cut it off and cast it from you; for it is more profitable for you that one of your members perish, than for your whole body to be cast into hell.* (Matt. 5:27-30)

There may be something wrong in our spirits when there is lack of joy, peace, security, and boldness. On the positive side, when we are walking in the fear of the Lord and in right relationship with Him, we experience a holy joy and boldness. Our sins are "covered" and "washed" away by the blood of Christ. We are in spiritual health. We can see God without fear or shame because of the blood of Christ (II Tim. 2:21). Those who practice sexual sin as a lifestyle cannot enter into the Kingdom of God (I Cor. 6:9,10).

## SPIRITUAL WARFARE[22]

## ARMOR OF GOD

1. Loins girded about with Truth: I Peter 1:13; John 8:44 (Satan the father of lies)
2. Breastplate of Righteousness: Self (Isa. 64:6) – Imparted (Eph. 5:9)
3. Rom. 8:4; II Tim. 2:22: Imputed (Rom. 3:24,25)
4. Gospel of Peace: I Pet. 3:15 – for defense and proclamation of the Gospel of Peace.
5. Shield of Faith (covers the whole body): I John 5;4,5; Heb. 11:1
6. I Tim. 6:11,12; II Tim. 1:13

---

[22] Eph. 6:10-18

7. Helmet of Salvation (absolute assurance of victory): I Thess. 5:8; I Pet. 1:5; Isa. 59:17; John 10:27-29
8. Sword of the Spirit: Matt. 4:1-11; Heb. 4:12, 13
9. Praying in the Spirit: Matt. 26:41; Mark 13:33; Eph. 1:16
10. Always: Luke 18:1; I Thess. 5:17; Rom. 12:12
11. In the Spirit: Rom. 8:26; Jude 20; Eph. 2:18; John 4:24
    - Temptations to lust – precautions with men/women – flee youthful lusts
    - II Cor. 10:4-5 – fleshly wisdom or human reasoning, rationalizations, theories, proud and lofty things ... all demonic in origin
    - High ideas of self; stand bare and naked with God's armor ALONE!!
    - Col. 1:14, 15 – Christ the Conqueror (Cross defeated): Heb. 2:14,15; I Pet. 3:18, 22
    - Luke 10:18 – Satan already falling from heaven
    - End – Rev. 20 – lake of fire

We are told to resist the devil and he will flee from you. We are not to give place to the devil. Again, we are told to put on the whole armor of God that we might be able to stand against the attacks of the evil one (Eph. 6:10-18; James 4:7; I Pet. 5:8-10). We stand in victory, not in fear! You are cleansed by the blood of Christ (Rev. 12:10). He has chosen you and sealed you. No one can pluck you out of God's hand (John 10:28,29).

## **JESUS CHRIST IS THE VICTOR!**[23]

*The Son of Man came to destroy the work of the devil. (I John 3:8)*

*He canceled the record of the charges against us and took it away by nailing it to the Cross. In this way, He disarmed the spiritual rulers and authorities. He shamed them publicly by His victory over them on the Cross. (Col. 2:14, NLT)*

*How God anointed Jesus of Nazareth with the Holy Spirit and with power, who went about doing good and healing all who were oppressed by the devil, for God was with Him. (Acts 10:38)*

---

[23] I John 3:8; Heb. 2:14, 15; Col. 1:15; I Cor. 15:55; Heb. 1:3; Eph. 1:21; Matt. 16:18; Rev. 20:1-3; Matt. 16:8,19

> *Inasmuch then as the children have partaken of flesh and blood, He Himself likewise shared in the same, that through death He might destroy him who had the power of death, that is, the devil. (Heb. 2:14)*

The Kingdom of Christ shall prevail. **Greater is He that is in you than he that is in the world** (I John 4:4). The **prince of this world** has been defeated. The **god of this world** has been overthrown at the Cross. The world, "under the power of the evil one" and the ruler of the power of the air, the enemy of those planting seeds in mission, has been defeated! Christ has overcome. He is the Ruler, the King of Kings, and Lord of Lords. He has won the victory and we need not fear. Yes, we will be continually attacked, harassed, tempted, and persecuted. But, **this is the victory that overcomes the world, even our faith** (I John 5:4). The Land of Canaan has been given. We are to possess the land by warfare.

The Bible says that **they overcame Satan by the blood of the Lamb, and by the word of their testimony** (Rev. 12:11). Christ is the Conqueror. Again, the Cross defeated Satan. The blood took away Satan's authority. He still can "roar," but His teeth have been taken out! Hallelujah!

> *I am not a sinner who struggles to love God.*
> *I am primarily a lover of God who struggles with sin!*

> *For no temptation (no trial regarded as enticing to sin), [no matter how it comes or where it leads] has overtaken you and laid hold on you that is not common to man [that is, no temptation or trial has come to you that is beyond human resistance and that is not adjusted and adapted and belonging to human experience, and such as man can bear]. But God is faithful [to His Word and to His compassionate nature], and He [can be trusted] not to let you be tempted and tried and assayed beyond your ability and strength of resistance and power to endure, but with the temptation He will [always] also provide the way out (the means of escape to a landing place), that you may be capable and strong and powerful to bear up under it patiently.*
> *(I Corinthians 10:13 - AMP)*

# CHAPTER TWELVE

# Suffering

When we follow Jesus as our Model Missionary, we are promised we will experience suffering.

> *For to this you were called, because Christ also suffered for us, leaving us an example, that you should follow His steps. (1 Peter 2:21)*

Jesus suffered! He was **slain before the foundation of the world** (Rev. 13:8). He suffered while He was here on earth and drank the final *cup* of suffering on the Cross (Matt. 20:23). He promised suffering to His followers when He was here on earth (Matt. 5:11,12). In John 15:20, Jesus predicted that the **whole world will hate you and that in this world you will have trials, tribulations, and distress** (John 16:33; Luke 6:22). To follow Christ is to be called to suffering (John 20:21). Some in the world will kill and persecute you (Matt. 10:16; Luke 11:49). He also gave the promise of a **great reward in heaven** for the persecuted (Matt. 5:12).

Therefore, we should not be surprised then when we suffer (Luke 11:49). The Gospel spreads through persecution (Acts 8:1,4; 11:19; 14:5,6; Phil. 1:4; I Thess. 1:6,7). In Jesus' promise of the Baptism in the Holy Spirit, the disciples would be a **witness unto Me**. The word **witness** in the original Greek language is the word **maturion**—"martyr" (Acts 1:8). The history of the Church down through the ages has testified to that truth. It is estimated that thousands die for their faith annually—more in this century than all the centuries before.

## A. PROMISED [24]

When we follow Jesus as our Model Missionary, we are promised persecution.

> *Therefore, since Christ has suffered in the flesh, arm yourselves also with the same purpose, because he who has suffered in the flesh has ceased*

---

[24] Mark 13:9-13; Luke 21:12-17; Matt. 10:16; Luke 11:49; Mark 8:31 cf. Luke 17:25

> *from sin. Beloved, do not think it strange concerning the fiery trial which is to try you, as though some strange thing happened to you; but rejoice to the extent that you partake of Christ's sufferings, that when His glory is revealed, you may also be glad with exceeding joy. If you are reproached for the name of Christ, blessed are you, for the Spirit of glory and of God rests upon you. (1 Peter 4:1-14)*

Jesus promised it to the Church. Some people endure suffering in a much greater way than others, and some endure it in different ways than in physical persecution. Jesus predicted that we would be persecuted and prosecuted ... hated ... brought before the courts ... and martyred.

## ILLUSTRATION

Chet Bitterman, a missionary with Wycliffe, was killed by guerillas in 1981 in Columbia. There were double the applications to Wycliffe Bible Translators following his death (Luke 10:3; Mark 10:39; 13:9; John 17;14; Acts 14:22; I Thess. 3;3; II Tim. 3:12).

> *If the world hates you, you know that it hated Me before it hated you. If you were of the world, the world would love its own. Yet because you are not of the world, but I chose you out of the world, therefore the world hates you. The servant is not greater than his Lord ... if they have persecuted Me, they will persecute you also. (John 15:18-21)* [25]

Jesus not only promised it, but says that we are to rejoice and be glad in it! Only by the Spirit of God can this happen in us. He is the One who gives us the desire and the joy to endure suffering for His Name's sake and for His glory.

> *Blessed are those who have been persecuted for the sake of righteousness, for theirs is the kingdom of heaven. Blessed are you when people insult you and persecute you, and falsely say all kinds of evil against you because of Me. Rejoice and be glad, for your reward in heaven is great; for in the same way they persecuted the prophets who were before you. (Matt 5:10-12, NASB)*

---

[25] I Peter 4:12-16

## GOD'S GLORIOUS PROMISE OF HIS LOVE AND CARE

> *Who shall separate us from the love of Christ? Shall trouble or hardship or persecution or famine or nakedness or danger or sword? As it is written: "For your sake we face death all day long; we are considered as sheep to be slaughtered." No, in all these things we are more than conquerors through him who loved us. For I am convinced that neither death nor life, neither angels nor demons, neither the present nor the future, nor any powers, neither height nor depth, nor anything else in all creation, will be able to separate us from the love of God that is in Christ Jesus our Lord. (Rom. 8:35-39, NIV)*

Christ's response while here on earth was love not hatred, rather the sacrificing of self for others. Christ would send his disciples with the same method—the Cross! These things would be achieved by death of the martyrs. It will achieve the triumph of God's truth, the ultimate defeat of Satan, and bring glory to God. God used the suffering of the church to scatter missionaries to other parts of the world (Acts 8:1). At that time, the church was only in Jerusalem.

> *Meanwhile, the believers who had been scattered during the persecution after Stephen's death traveled as far as Phoenicia, Cyprus, and Antioch of Syria. They preached the word of God, but only to Jews. (Acts 11:19, NLT)*

God even used imprisonments to further the cause of missions—and still does today.

> *But before all these things, they will lay their hands on you and will persecute you, delivering you to the synagogues and prisons, bringing you before kings and governors for My name's sake. It will lead to an opportunity for your testimony. (Luke 21:12,13,s)*

---

> The extent of our sacrifice coupled with the depth of our joy displays the worth we put on the reward of God. Loss and suffering joyfully accepted, for the Kingdom of God, show the supremacy of God's glory more clearly in the worth than all worship and prayer." —John Piper

---

We are encouraged to hold fast our profession of faith. He has gone before us. He understands what we are going through. He is our strength in our persecution. He sympathizes with us. We come to the throne of grace fearlessly and boldly to find help in the time of need (Heb. 4:14-16). When God sent His Son into the world it was prophesied that He would suffer and be crucified. He expects us to meet the same hatred, violence, even death. As we mentioned to you, Acts 1:8 says that you shall receive power to be *"**martyrs**."* Here is what happened to the disciples.

- James, son of Zebedee – killed by the sword
- Peter – crucified (possibly upside down—not worthy to be crucified like His Lord)
- Andrew – crucified
- Matthias – stoned in Jerusalem and then beheaded
- James, the son of Alpheus – crucified
- Philip – scourged, thrown into prison, and then crucified
- Simeon – crucified
- Thaddeus – killed by arrows
- James, brother of Jesus – at 94, brains bashed out
- Thomas – killed by the sword
- Bartholomew – beaten and crucified in India
- Mark – dragged and cut to pieces in front of pagan idol, Serapes
- Stephen – stoned
- Luke – hanged on an olive tree
- Paul – jailed and then beheaded
- John, the "beloved disciple" – put into a pot of hot, boiling oil. By a miracle of God, he was taken out without any injury! Domitian, the Roman governor, immediately banished him to the Isle of Patmos, where John wrote the book of Revelation. He is the only disciple of Christ to escape violent death.

*Don't forget about those in prison. Suffer with them as though you were there yourself. Share the sorrow of those being mistreated, as though you feel their pain in your own bodies. (Heb. 13:3 NLT)*

*A disciple is not above his teacher, nor a servant above his master. It is enough for a disciple that he be like his teacher, and a servant like his master. If they have called the master of the house Beelzebub, how much more will they call those of his household! (Matt. 10:24,25)*

Matt. 21:12; Mark 10:39 – *drink the cup of betrayal*; 13:9 – *they will deliver you up* (Matt. 5:10-12) I Peter 4:12-19 – *think it not strange concerning the fiery trial ... rejoice for you are partners of Christ's suffering*; Heb. 4:14-16; Matt. 10:16-42 (read); John 16:2 – *they will kill you and think they do God's service;* Matt. 24:9 – *they shall deliver you up to tribulation and put you to death and you will be hated by all nations for My Name's sake.* (Matt. 10:16-20; I Thess. 3:2,3; John 20:20; 15:20)

> *For what credit is there if, when you sin and are harshly treated, you endure it with patience? But if when you do what is right and suffer for it you patiently endure it, this finds favor with God. For you have been called for this purpose, since Christ also suffered for you, leaving you an example for you to follow in His steps. (1 Peter 2:20-21, NASB)*

There are hundreds of martyrs every day for their faith around the world. Some estimate that there are more martyrs for Christ in this century than all the centuries preceding. According to Gordon-Conwell, 159,000 martyrs die each year for Christ. The *International Bulletin of Missionary Research* says that there may be even more and they project that by 2025, 210,000 Christians will die annually! It is estimated by some that hundreds die for their faith every week, unknown and unreported, but well known to God! Most are unknown to man, but they are well known to God, awaiting the resurrection! *Christ Is Our Example: Don't Be Surprised!*

## B. PRESENCE OF POWER[26]

> *But you shall receive power when the Holy Spirit has come upon you; and you shall be witnesses [martyrs] to Me in Jerusalem, and in all Judea and Samaria, and to the end of the earth. (Acts 1:8)*

> *When you are arrested, don't worry about how to respond or what to say. God will give you the right words at the right time. For it is not you who will be speaking—it will be the Spirit of your Father speaking through you. (Matt. 10:19,20, NLT)*

> *For God has not given us a spirit of fear, but of power and of love and of a sound mind. (I Tim 1:7)*

---

[26] Col. 1:11

## C. CHURCH GROWTH[27]

The Early Church experienced explosive growth through much persecution. Stephen was stoned while Paul watched (Act 7:54-60). Because of stoning of Stephen, Paul is stoned and flees to another city (Acts 11:19). There he preaches the Gospel (Acts 14:19-23). Sudan lost 2 million in the last 11 years. There are about 5,000 new churches as a result!

> *Therefore those who were scattered went everywhere preaching the word. (Acts 8:4)*

> *Now those who were scattered after the persecution that arose over Stephen traveled as far as Phoenicia, Cyprus, and Antioch, preaching the word to no one but the Jews only. (Acts 11:19)*

Paul prays for the church that they would be **strengthened with all might, according to His glorious power, for all patience and longsuffering with joy** (Col. 1:11). Paul asks the church to pray *that* **we may be delivered from unreasonable and wicked men; for not all have faith** (II Thess. 3:2).

> *Remember the prisoners as if chained with them—those who are mistreated—since you yourselves are in the body also. (Heb. 13:3)*

I can say that it is easier to teach about it than go through it. Sometimes I weep for those who are suffering and dying for their faith. I would ask that I would be able to receive His grace should that ever happen to me. The Bible reminds us to identify with them.

Our purpose is not to die but to make Christ known in the world in life or in death. Polycarp (A.D. 70-155) was arrested for his faith. Being elderly, the Romans asked that he repeat, even quietly, "Caesar is Lord." He refused. His response: **"Eighty-six years I have served Christ, and He never did me any wrong. How can I blaspheme my King who saved me?"**

Steadfast in his stand for Christ, Polycarp refused to compromise his beliefs, and thus, was burned alive at the stake. Thousands have given the same testimony in different situations with different words with the same ending—martyrdom!

---

[27] Acts 8:1,4; 11:19; 14:5-7

## ILLUSTRATION

Koreans fled to North Korea as Japan invaded in the 1930s. Many also went to Vladivostok, Russia. Stalin intended to use them at weapons factories. He moved the Koreans to five different areas in the Soviet Union. Many were sent to Tashkent, a Muslim hub of Uzbeks who had violently resisted the Gospel for years. Koreans became part of every facet of Uzbek cultural life. Believers began bringing their friends to Christ. In 1990 the first open-air Christian meeting in the history of Soviet Central Asia took place.

## OUR ATTITUDE

We are *blessed ... rejoice and be exceedingly glad for great is your reward in heaven* (Matt. 5:10-12; I Pet. 3:14, rejoice; I Pet. 4:12-14, happy; John 14:27, peace).

> *But I say, <u>love</u> your enemies! <u>Pray</u> for those who persecute you! In that way, you will be acting as true children of your Father in heaven. (Matt. 5:44,45)*

> *Beloved, do not think it strange concerning the fiery trial which is to try you, as though some strange thing happened to you; but rejoice to the extent that you partake of Christ's sufferings, that when His glory is revealed, you may also be glad with exceeding joy. (I Peter 4:12,13, NLT)*

> *Not only so, but we also rejoice in our sufferings. (Rom. 5:3, NIV)*

> *Love your enemies! <u>Pray</u> for those who persecute you! (Matt. 5:44)*

> *Blessed are you when men hate you, And when they exclude you, And revile you, and cast out your name as evil, for the Son of Man's sake. Rejoice in that day and leap for joy! For indeed your reward is great in heaven, for in like manner their fathers did to the prophets. (Luke 6:22,23)*

> *They departed from the presence of the council, rejoicing that they were counted worthy to suffer shame for His name. (Acts 5:41)*

> *That I may know Him and the power of His resurrection, and the fellowship of His sufferings, being conformed to His death ... (Phil. 3:10)*

> *Who shall separate us from the love of Christ? Shall tribulation, or distress, or persecution, or famine, or nakedness, or peril, or sword? As it is written: "For Your sake we are killed all day long; We are accounted as sheep for the slaughter." Yet in all these things we are more than conquerors through Him who loved us. For I am persuaded that neither death nor life, nor angels nor principalities nor powers, nor things present nor things to come, nor height nor depth, nor any other created thing, shall be able to separate us from the love of God which is in Christ Jesus our Lord. (Rom. 8:35-39)*

---

Suffering with joy proves to the world that our Treasure is in heaven, not on earth, and that this Treasure is greater than anything the world has to offer. The supremacy of God's worth shines through the pain that His people gladly bear for His Name. God is worth more than all earthly treasures, including life itself.

—John Piper, *Let the Nations Be Glad*

---

## D. REWARDS

Matthew 5:11, 12; Luke 6:22, 23; II Corinthians 4:16-18; James 1:12; I Corinthians 9:25; II Timothy 4:8 (***crown of righteousness***); I Peter 4:14 (***spirit of glory and of God rests upon you***); Philippians 3:10; Romans 8:17 (***if we suffer with Him, we shall also be glorified together***); I Peter 5:10 (***make you perfect, settle, strengthen you***).

> *Blessed are those who are persecuted for righteousness' sake, for theirs is the kingdom of heaven. Blessed are you when they revile and persecute you, and say all kinds of evil against you falsely for My sake. Rejoice and be exceedingly glad, for great is your reward in heaven, for so they persecuted the prophets who were before you. (Matt. 5:10-12)*

> *Peter began to say to Him, "Behold, we have left everything and followed You." Jesus said, "Truly I say to you, there is no one who has left house or brothers or sisters or mother or father or children or farms, for My sake and for the gospel's sake, but that he will receive a hundred times as much now in the present age, houses and brothers and sisters and mothers and children and farms, along with persecutions; and in*

> the age to come, eternal life. "But many who are first will be last, and the last, first." (Mark 10:28-31, NASB)[28]

Jesus acknowledged that allegiance to Him and the Gospel (Matt. 8:35) is a break with old ties of home, loved ones, or property (fields), as the case may be (cf. 13:11-13; Luke 9:59-62). But, to everyone who makes the break, Jesus promised that all these things will be replaced a hundredfold by new ties with fellow disciples The items enumerated here may be taken literally to refer to such things as the many homes which will be opened to God's servants and the many new relationships in the household of God (I Pet. 4:14; Phil. 3:10; Luke 19:17; Matt. 25:21).

> *Blessed are you when men hate you, And when they exclude you, And revile you, and cast out your name as evil, for the Son of Man's sake. Rejoice in that day and leap for joy! For indeed your reward is great in heaven, For in like manner their fathers did to the prophets. (Luke 6:22,23)*

> *... and when the Chief Shepherd appears, you will receive the crown of glory that does not fade away. (I Peter 5:4)*

> *If you are reproached for the name of Christ, blessed are you, for the Spirit of glory and of God rests upon you. On their part He is blasphemed, but on your part He is glorified. (I Peter 4:14)*

## CONCLUDING NOTE

Jesus suffered! He was **slain before the foundation of the world** (Rev. 13:8). He suffered while He was here on earth and drank the final cup of suffering on the Cross (Matt. 20:23). He promised suffering to His followers when He was here on earth (Matt. 5:11,12). In John 15:21, Jesus predicted that the **whole world will hate you** and that **in this world you will have trials, tribulations, and distress** (John 16:33; Luke 6:22). He also gave the promise of a **great reward in heaven** for the persecuted. Therefore, we should not be surprised when we suffer (Luke 11:49). The Gospel spreads through persecution (Acts 8:1,4; 11:19; 14:5,6; Phil. 1:4; I Thess. 1:6, 7). In Jesus' promise of the baptism in the Holy Spirit, the disciples would be a witness unto Me. The word in the original language is the word **maturion**—martyr

---

[28] Phil. 3:7-10; I Pet. 5:4

(Acts 1:8). The history of the Church down through the ages has testified to that truth. It is estimated that thousands die for their faith annually.

## ILLUSTRATION

J. Oswald Sanders tells the story of an indigenous missionary who walked barefoot from village to village preaching the gospel in India. After a long day of many miles and much discouragement, he came to a certain village and tried to speak the gospel but was spurned. So he went to the edge of the village dejected, lay down under a tree, and slept from exhaustion.

When he awoke, the whole town was gathered to hear him. The head man of the village explained that they had looked him over while he was sleeping. When they saw his blistered feet, they concluded that he must be a holy man and that they had been evil to reject him. They were sorry and wanted to hear the message for which he was willing to suffer so much to bring them (*Let the Nations be Glad*, Piper, p. 92).

# PART THREE

# Chapter One

# Resurrection and Ascension

Christianity stands or falls with the Resurrection of Christ. Without it, we have platitudes. The miracles become false, a myth, and *we are of men most miserable* (I Cor. 15:16-19). However, there is more evidence for the Resurrection of Christ than for the death of Socrates! There is direct connection between the Resurrection and our mission. The angel expressed to Mary Magdalene on the first Easter day, *Do not be afraid ... He is not here ... come and see ... go and tell ...* (Mark 16:1-8). The Church has seen and is telling of Christ's Death and Resurrection ever since. That is the Gospel, the Good News. The first recorded words of Jesus to His disciples after His Resurrection were, *Peace be with you. As the Father has sent Me, even so I am sending you* (John 20:21). The Resurrection not only brought peace but joy and boldness (Acts 4:13,29; 5:40-42; 15:26).

The Crucifixion and the Resurrection are necessarily linked together. Without the Resurrection there would be no salvation—*raised again for our justification* (Rom. 4:25; I Cor. 15:3,4; 2:1-5). Saving faith includes belief in the Resurrection (***Rom. 10:9-10: that if you confess with your mouth the Lord Jesus and believe in your heart that God has raised Him from the dead, you will be saved. For with the heart one believes unto righteousness, and with the mouth confession is made unto salvation,*** **NKJV**). The truth brings comfort with hope (I Thess. 4:14). If Christ did not rise from the dead we are *most miserable and to be pitied* (I Cor. 15:12-20). Christ is risen indeed!

> *... that if you confess with your mouth the Lord Jesus and believe in your heart that God has raised Him from the dead, you will be saved. For with the heart one believes unto righteousness, and with the mouth confession is made unto salvation. (Rom. 10:9,10)*

1. EVIDENCE OF THE RESURRECTION

    1. **Jesus' own Testimony**

        *From that time Jesus began to show to His disciples that He must go to Jerusalem, and suffer many things from the elders and chief priests and scribes, and be killed, and be raised the third day. (Luke 9:21)*

    2. **Prophesied** as a Proof of His Deity in Old and New Testaments (Matt. 26:32)

        *But after I am risen again, I will go before you into Galilee; destroy this Temple, and in three days I will raise it up. (Mark 9:9; John 2:19)*

        *Neither will you allow your Holy One to see corruption. (Psa. 16:10; Acts 2:31)*

    3. **Empty Tomb**—Matt. 28:1-6; Luke 24:3,12; John 20:1, 2 (guarded by Roman soldiers, the stone of nearly two tons rolled away)
    4. **Grave Clothes**—unmoved and still bound together
    5. **Eye Witnesses**—Matt. 28:6,8-10; Mark 16:6 (an angel at the tomb speaks); John 20:19,26 (Jesus speaks); seen by 500 at one time (I Cor. 15:6).

        *... to whom He also presented Himself alive after His suffering by many infallible proofs, being seen by them during forty days and speaking of the things pertaining to the kingdom of God. "Therefore, of these men who have accompanied us all the time that the Lord Jesus went in and out among us, beginning from the baptism of John to that day when He was taken up from us, one of these must become a witness with us of His resurrection." (Acts 1:3,21,22)*

    6. **Appearances**—John 20:19-26; Luke 24:34-39 (same body as before); Matt. 28:16,17; I Cor. 15:1-8 (500 at one time)
    7. **Christian Church** is a result
    8. **Moral transformation of disciples**: from timid to bold proclaimers of the truth
    9. **Calendar**: After Christ (A.D. – "the year of the Lord")
    10. **Change from Saturday worship to Sunday**
    11. **Josephus**: Jewish historian (not a Christian) states that Jesus rose again

12. **No denials under persecution**
13. **Personal Experiences** – people seeing Christ in dreams even today (Muslims and others)
14. **Christ continuing His Work testifying to His resurrection**
15. **Pentecost**: The apostles were witnesses, and their witness was effective because it was accompanied by power!

## ASCENSION: JESUS RETURNS TO HIS FATHER'S HOUSE

*I go to prepare a place for you ... I go to the Father ... I came from the Father ... I leave the world, and go to the Father ...(John 14:2)*

As the Cross is incomplete without the Resurrection, so the Resurrection would be incomplete without the **Ascension**. It was after the **Ascension** that Christ promised the Church would receive the Spirit in a new dimension at Pentecost (John 7:37-39; 16:7; Acts 2:32,33). It was in the **Ascension** of Christ that the Father gave all authority to the Son, who now gives it to His Church (Matt. 28:18-20). It is only in the **Ascension** that Christ is interceding for us and pleading the cause of missions with the Father as our High Priest and Advocate (Heb. 7:24,25; Rom. 8:34; I John 2:2). It is only with the **Ascension** that Christ gives gifts to the Church to fulfill His global mission (Eph. 4:11,12). God has highly exalted Him ... and *that every tongue should confess that Jesus Christ is Lord to the glory of God the Father* (Phil. 2:8-11; Rev. 11:15; 19:1-6,22).

*... taken up into glory ... (I Tim. 3:16)*

*... sit on the right hand until I make your enemies a footstool for your feet ... (Psa. 110:1)*

*Father, glorify Me with the glory I had before ... (John 17:5)*

The **Ascension** marked the beginning of Christ's intercession for His followers at the right hand of God. There He makes continual intercession for all believers (Rom. 8:34; Heb. 4:14; 6:20; 7:25). Although Christ is not physically present with His people today, He is no less concerned for them or less active on their behalf. Christians enjoy peace, hope, and security because Christ is their advocate with the Father (1 John 2:1).

The **Ascension** set in motion the coming of the Holy Spirit with His gifts for believers (John 14:16-18,26; 16:7-15; Acts 2:23; Eph. 4:11,12). God determined that the presence of Jesus would be replaced by the presence of the Holy Spirit, who could be everywhere at the same time. Jesus' followers now enjoy the presence of the Spirit and the operation of the Spirit's gifts through them.

One additional result of the ascension is that Jesus began His heavenly reign at the right hand of the Father (I Cor. 15:20-28). This reign will last until His **SECOND COMING**, when He will return to the earth as the reigning Messiah (Acts 3:20,21).

Finally, the **ascension** of Christ is the pledge of His second coming: ***This same Jesus, who was taken up from you into heaven, will so come in like manner as you saw Him go into heaven*** (Acts 1:11). Jesus will return to earth in bodily form just as He ascended into heaven.

# Chapter Two

# Second Coming and Missions

The chief task, privilege, and joy Christ has given the Church is to proclaim the universal lordship of Christ until He returns. Why does the Lord wait so long? He gives us one reason. He is **not willing that any should perish but that all should come to repentance** (II Pet. 3:9). Each day that Christ postpones His return, thousands are being converted to Christ and other millions are being presented the Gospel through preaching, literature distribution, radio, television, the Internet, and personal witness.

> *And this gospel of the kingdom will be preached in all the world as a witness to all the nations, and then the end will come. (Matt. 24:14)*

> *But, beloved, do not forget this one thing, that with the Lord one day is as a thousand years, and a thousand years as one day. The Lord is not slack concerning His promise [of His return], as some count slackness, but is longsuffering toward us, not willing that any should perish but that all should come to repentance. But the day of the Lord will come as a thief in the night ... (II Peter 3:8-10)*

In Psalm 2:8 the decree of the Father to His Son is that the Son should *ask of Me and I will give the nations as Thine inheritance.* Revelation 5:9 and 7:9 identify this inheritance as those purchased for God with *Thy blood, from every tribe and tongue and people and nation.*

Romans 11:25-32 maintains that the salvation of the nation of Israel and the coming of the Kingdom to earth wait **until the fullness of the Gentiles has come in**. The prophetic "time clock" of Daniel 9:24-27 and Acts 1:6-8 for the Kingdom of God to come to earth waits for the completion of the Church as the Bride and Body of Christ. There needs to be representation in the Bride and Body of Christ from **"every tribe, tongue, people, and nation."**

## UNTO THE ENDS OF THE EARTH

> *But you shall receive power when the Holy Spirit has come upon you; and you shall be witnesses to Me in Jerusalem, and in all Judea and Samaria, and to the end of the earth. (Acts 1:8)*

Christ not only commissioned the Church to continue its mandate to proclaim the Gospel *to the end of the age* (Matt. 28:20)—not the apostolic age only—but also to *the ends of the earth* (Acts 1:8). *The earth is the Lord's and the fullness thereof, the world and all who dwell therein* (Psa. 24:1). *His Kingdom rules over all* (Psa. 103:19; Acts 17:31; John 5:29; Matt. 25:32; John 3:17). Jesus is *the Savior of all men* (I Tim. 4:10; I John 4:14), *the field is the world* (Matt. 13:38), and *that if He would be lifted up, He would draw all men unto Himself* (John 12:32). It is the world which is the heart of the Gospel (John 3:16) *and whosoever calls on the name of the Lord shall be saved* (Rom. 10:13).

We know when Christ is coming—not the day nor the hour, but *when this Gospel of the Kingdom shall be preached to all the ethnic groups of the world, then shall the end come* (Matt. 24:14). There will be people from every ethnic group, tongue, peoples, and nations (Rev. 5:9). Christ shall return to earth, the Church will be raptured, and its work on earth will be completed. Second Peter 3:1-12 seems to indicate we can hasten the coming of Christ, by reaching to those perishing that they would come to repentance. Also, the Bride has made herself ready (Matt. 24:14).

## THE MISSION OF CHRIST SHALL SUCCEED!

> *After these things I looked, and behold, a great multitude which no one could number, of all nations, tribes, peoples, and tongues, standing before the throne and before the Lamb, clothed with white robes with palm branches in their hands. (Rev. 7:9)*

> *They will come from the east and the west, from the north and the south, and sit down in the kingdom of God. (Luke 13:29)*

> *And then He will send His angels, and gather together His elect from the four winds, from the farthest part of earth to the farthest part of heaven. (Mark 13:27)*

> *And they sang a new song with these words: "You are worthy to take the scroll and break its seals and open it. For you were slaughtered,*

> and your blood has ransomed people for God from every tribe and
> language and people and nation. And you have caused them to become
> a Kingdom of priests for our God. And they will reign on the earth.
> (Rev. 5:9-10, NLT)

## **ETERNITY**

Missions began in eternity and will end in eternity. We must keep eternity in mind. This world is not our home. We are just passing through. Only what is done with and for Christ will last.

## **CHALLENGE**

> *Therefore we make it our aim, whether present or absent, to be well pleasing to Him. For we must all appear before the judgment seat of Christ, that each one may receive the things done in the body, according to what he has done, whether good or bad. Knowing, therefore, the terror of the Lord, we persuade men; but we are well known to God, and I also trust are well known in your consciences. (II Cor. 5:9-11)*

You are a special person in the Body of Christ. You have been called of God to make Him known through you. Every member is part of the whole Body. We give more honor to the visible, but without the invisible, we could not have the visible! You will not be rewarded for how many seeds you have sown or the results, but because you have been a good and faithful servant.

> *Well done, good and faithful servant. You have been faithful over a little: I will set you over much. Enter into the joy of your Master.* (Matt. 25:21)

## **SOME CONCLUSIONS**

From a human point of view at the time of Christ, the ministry of Jesus was not successful. The religious leaders rejected him, He was accused of being demon possessed, some tried to kill Him, most of the people only followed Him for the miracles and His feeding them, He was misunderstood and ridiculed, the nation of Israel rejected Him, His own twelve disciples all forsook Him, and finally He was crucified naked on the Cross alone between two thieves, even abandoned by His Father! What a picture of despair and failure! Yet, He was faithful to His mission—sowing the Seed of His life. He was faithful in declaring the Message and love of His Father. The circumstances never kept Him from following His call and the purpose of His coming! His motivation was not to be successful, but to be obedient and faithful.

The Resurrection and the Ascension were God's answer to His Son's faithful obedience through suffering! ***Who for the joy that was set before Him, endured the Cross*** and suffering (Heb. 12:1-3). He could see the reward of His labor—the Church, His Bride!

Christ has called the Church to do the same—to be faithful and obedient, not necessarily successful from the human point of view. Christ is in us, the Hope of Glory. It is His Life that we are to express. He has appointed the Church to go and bear fruit and that fruit would remain, so that whatsoever we ask the Father in His Name, the Father would give it to us (John 15:16). Missions is not a ministry of the Church. It is *the* ministry of the Church. We deny the world the blessings of Christ and His salvation when we do not respond to Christ's command. God desires worshipers. We follow Christ who came to seek and to save the lost. He promises to baptize us with power to be His witnesses and to be with us, even to the end of the age (Acts 1:8; Matt. 28:20). He has promised that greater works shall we do, because He goes to the Father and that signs and wonders shall follow those that believe (John 14:12-18; Mark 16:15-18). Jesus is calling us to *run the race that is set before us,* ***looking unto Jesus, the Author and Finisher of our faith*** (Heb. 12:2). Let us go forward following the victorious Christ until He comes again!

## **UNFINISHED TASK**

The Church has done more in terms of missions outreach in the last one-half century than in all the years since the Apostolic Age. With modern technology, printing, airplanes, Internet, automobiles, television, radio, films, etc., the Gospel has been spread around the world. There are yet many closed doors, but there are also many open doors to the Gospel. Christ has not come. When will He come? One reason He has not come is because the Gospel of the Kingdom has not yet been preached to all nations (Mark 13:10). We can hasten the Lord's return by sharing our passion for the glory of God in the world ... to have more worshipers added to the throng in heaven which no man can number.

According to the Joshua Project, there are approximately 16,650 people groups (those with a specific language, culture, and background that would make them distinct from others). There are yet 7,183 people groups unreached with the Gospel (43.1%). **Unreached** means *"that there is not a known indigenous (native) community of Bible believers large enough to evangelize this group."* The great pastor and missionary, Dr. Oswald Smith, once posed a question: *Is it right for people to hear the Gospel twice, if there are still those who haven't heard it once?* (www.joshuaproject.net)

We cannot change the world, but we are to love Christ and His Return enough to be a part of God's end-time harvest. We are not pessimists. The Kingdom of God is advancing, in spite of the worldwide opposition of the enemy. The *gates of hell shall not prevail* against Christ and His Kingdom. The final Victory is assured.

Let us hasten His Return (II Peter 3:12). Let us make ourselves fully available to follow the Lamb and Lord of the Harvest. With my passion for Him and His glory, I will surrender myself wholly to His Lordship to follow Him, by His grace and power of the Spirit. I will do whatever He asks me to do, go wherever He wishes me to go, and say whatever He asks me to say. It will be worth it all when we hear His *Well done, good and faithful servant*. (Matt. 25:21) Let us again be continually filled with the Holy Spirit. We shall be rewarded abundantly by His grace (Luke 18:28-30). Christ's payer shall be answered (John 17:20-21), and His mission shall succeed (Matt. 24:14).

> *And this Gospel of the Kingdom will be proclaimed through the whole world as a testimony to all nations, and then the end will come. (Mat. 24:14 –ESV)*
>
> *I do not ask for these only, but also for them who will believe in Me through their word, that they may all be one, just as you, Father, are in Me, and I in you. John 17:20, 21 - ESV)*
>
> *The Lord is not slack concerning His promise, as some count slackness, but is longsuffering toward us, not willing that any should perish but that all should come to repentance. (II Peter 3:9)*

## QUESTION

Will you make yourself fully available to Him? Will you make yourself available in whatever way the Lord has spoken to you? When He calls, follow Him. It will be worth it all! Have you or are you willing to respond to the call of God in your life?

## *PRAYER!*

# Addendum I

# I Believe in Reincarnation

Christ has come to earth again, in His church, the reincarnation of Christ, in you and me!

> ... even the Spirit of Truth, for He dwells with you, and shall be **in you**. (John 14:17)

> ... Christ **in** you the Hope of Glory. (Col. 1:27)

> At that day you will know that I am in My Father, and you in Me, and **I in you**. (John 14:20)

> Jesus answered and said to him, "If anyone loves Me, he will keep My word; and My Father will love him, and We will come to him and **make Our home with him**." (John 14:23)

> And the glory which You gave Me I have given them, that they may be **one just as We are one: I in them, and You in Me**; that they may be made perfect in one, and that the world may know that You have sent Me, and have loved them as You have loved Me. (John 17:22)

> Do you not know that you are **the temple of God and that the Spirit of God dwells in you**? (I Cor. 3:16)

> I have been crucified with Christ; it is no longer I who live, but **Christ lives in me**; and the life which I now live in the flesh I live by faith in the Son of God, who loved me and gave Himself for me. (Gal. 2:20)

> ... in whom you also are being built together for a **dwelling place of God in the Spirit**. (Eph. 2:22)

> You are of God, little children, and have overcome them, because He who is in you is greater than he who is **in** the world. (1 John 4:4)

Are there any that are living the life of Christ? Of course. Some famous ones are Mother Teresa and Hudson Taylor who are examples of those who lived out the life of Christ in their lives. I believe in reincarnation. There are people reaching those with the AIDS epidemic in Africa where I have been. There are people reaching the slums, the drug addicts, those in the high places in government, in our Congress, judges, and in all levels of society. We identify! We are living out Christ in our lives. Christ is IN us!

What does it mean to be incarnational? What does it mean that Christ is in you? That Christ is to be seen in you? What does it mean to "make Christ present in our world?" What does it mean that to see the Church is to see Christ? Here are some examples of what it means:

It is Jesus feeding the poor, giving a cup of water in His name: *as you have done it to the least of these, you have done it unto Me.* It is visiting in prison. helping evacuees, sharing the message of the Gospel, and an overflow of the love of God in the Katrina and Rita hurricanes. It is His Church, the fullness of Christ that is responding to Christ within—in His Name, even as Jesus, who not only preached, but went about doing good (Acts 10:38), healing and feeding.

When our life is committed to Christ, all we do is for His Name and for His glory, as Mother Teresa and her Sisters of Mercy, as Wilem and Mariet Brasma (friends of ours) working with lepers in a Nepal leprosarium, as those who feed the hungry, care for the elderly. As those ministering to homosexuals with Exodus International, alcoholics in rescue missions, who rescue victims of child prostitution and slavery—the rescue ministry in Amsterdam (at one time over 30,000 prostitutes there)—sharing Christ in word and deed. It is Teen Challenge in over 150 countries of the world sharing Christ and rescuing the drug addicts, alcoholics, prostitutes, and the oppressed of the world, restoring lives destroyed by the devil.

It is Amy Carmichael, who in 1901 who was rescuing children from the corruption of temple service. These little girls were "married to the gods" during religious Hindu ceremonies and endured horrible abuse. She would often kidnap these little ones from the jaws of hell.

It is a priest named Pietro Barnardone. He was returning from a crusade when a leper approached him. He sprang from his horse and threw his arms around him, kissing him. He went home, piled his garments in a heap, except his shirt, and walked out into the snow, penniless and parentless. He burst into song: "I am born again."

It is Bob Pierce who was so deeply moved by the effects of the Korean War, he wrote in his Bible, "Let my heart be broken by the things that break the heart of God." He rescued unclaimed children eating out of trash cans and sleeping under cardboard. He founded World Vision and Samaritan's Purse. A friend said that his ministry was "as the spurting blood from Pierce's broken heart." His statement after visiting the Orient was, "The only measurement in assessing what we should be in the war was, 'Is this something Jesus would do? Something God would want done?'"

He is Christ in Assemblies of God pioneer missionaries Harry and Helen Waggoner, who lived among the lepers of India and nearly died as the incarnation of Christ. It is Christ in an Indian named Devaraj who brought hope from the indescribable slave trade also in India. It is thousands who are being martyred every year who are following Christ to the death of the Cross. It is the many unknowns in this world but well-known to God who are loving and serving Christ in some of the remote regions of the world as did David Livingston, mauled by a lion trying to establish a mission station in Africa.

It is H. B. Garlock who took great risks in going to Liberia, known as "the white man's grave." When surrounded by an angry tribe of cannibals, he was given permission by the witch doctor to speak, "Before we kill and eat you, you are permitted so speak." The Spirit gave him words to speak and when he had finished the witch doctor asked forgiveness on behalf of the tribe from trying to harm him.

It is preaching the word through Wycliffe Bible Translators in some remote part of the world, translating the Bible into the language of tribes and people groups. It is the ministry of Dick Foth and others to those in Washington, D.C., making Christ known in Bible studies, prayer, and personal discipleship.

It is Heidi Williams who served with Mother Teresa in the Home for the Dying in Calcutta (Halighat), India. It is washing rubber sheets, cleaning, serving, giving massages to some who weigh 50 pounds and who have been there 25 years or more. She writes, "Jesus waits for us to draw near to Him. It is so much easier to pass by. But then, what joy at the end of the time. When the costume is pulled aside and we see Jesus in that drunken person we helped or in the street kid we reached out to." She writes further, "As wonderful as it is to bring the Kingdom of God to the hollow places of the earth, even this is rubbish compared with the surpassing greatness of knowing Christ Jesus. Intimacy with Christ must be first. Without it, mission is empty and self-serving.... Without intimacy with Jesus, we have nothing to give away to others."

It is Christ through His Church, the Life of Christ. When did you see Me hungry (Matt. 25:37)? When you hold the hand of the dying, comfort the sick, sit quietly in a waiting room after an operation, helping the elderly and the depressed, when you sit with a drug addict going through withdrawals, when you share the Gospel, give godly counsel to the distressed, those with broken homes and marriages. It is when you help the needy, give a cup of cold water in His Name, when you stand for truth and righteousness as a minority… when you weep with those who weep and rejoice with those who rejoice, when you witness of Christ, knock on doors, preach, heal and manifest His Name. It is Christ IN you! You are the incarnation of Christ when you pray in His Name, pleading His cause for others. It is when you go next door or around the world to preach the Gospel or to your next door neighbor, or share the love and witness of Christ on our jobs or at school. It is whether we preach to crowds or to one, as Jesus did so many times. It is when you are silent with your voice, but speak volumes with your life. It is Christ IN you! You are the incarnation of Christ! Hallelujah!

We are the Body of Christ (John 14:17,28; 17:20; I Cor. 12:12-17; Eph. 4:4-12; Col, 1:27). It is Christ in you. I Corinthians 3:16 calls use the temple of God. Ephesians 2:22 says we are the habitation of God. The Church is the visible representation of Christ on earth. What the world sees in Christ is His Church, faltering and triumphant! Reincarnation—Christ on earth again!

# ADDENDUM II

# Are the heathen lost without Christ?

Can a person without Christ have eternal life? Can he/she experience forgiveness of sins and be guaranteed heaven without Christ? Let us look at what the Scripture says about the "heathen."

---

**Definition of "Heathen"**: (1) An unconverted member of a people or nation that does not acknowledge the God of the Bible. (2) An uncivilized or irreligious person.
—Webster's Dictionary

---

Let's look at the Scriptures.

## DEFINITION OF HEATHEN

We define "heathen" as an unconverted member of a people or nation that does not acknowledge the God of the Bible and Jesus Christ as Lord and Savior. Are they really lost and under the judgment of God, under His wrath? We have to look the Scriptures to tell us the sobering truth.[29]

All are under sin (Rom. 2:8; 3:9-19,23), in the flesh and unable to submit to God or please God (Rom. 8:7,8), natural and not spiritual (I Cor. 2:14-16), dead in trespasses and sin and children of wrath (Eph. 2:1-5) and under demonic forces (Eph. 6:12; II Cor. 4:4—the god of this world has blinded their minds), darkened and alienated (separated) from God and hard in heart (Eph. 4:17, 18; II Thess. 1:8-10).

---

[29] Rom. 1:18-32; 2:8; 3:23; 5:12; Eph. 2:1-3; 4:18; 6:12; I Thess. 1:8-10 Heb. 9:27

## 1) THEY WERE NOT BORN HEATHEN.

They became heathen when they deliberately gave up their knowledge of God (Rom. 1:21-23). We inherited Adam's nature and we have all have sinned (3:23). It was an act, a choice, though sin was inherited.

> *For the wrath of God is revealed from heaven against all ungodliness and unrighteousness of men, who suppress the truth in unrighteousness ... (Rom 1:18)*

## 2) THEY DID NOT LOSE ALL KNOWLEDGE OF GOD.

> *Because what may be known of God is manifest in them, for God has shown it to them. For since the creation of the world His invisible attributes are clearly seen, being understood by the things that are made, even His eternal power and Godhead, so that they are without excuse, because, although they knew God, they did not glorify Him as God, nor were thankful, but became futile in their thoughts, and their foolish hearts were darkened. (Rom. 1:19-21)*

They rejected the revelation they had. They have no excuse, even though they do not have the revelation others have. The Scriptures tell us that they are under demonic forces. Man rejects the true God and seeks a different god.

> *You used to live in sin, just like the rest of the world, obeying the devil—the commander of the powers in the unseen world. He is the spirit at work in the hearts of those who refuse to obey God. (Eph. 2:2, NLT)*

## 3) THE REVELATION OF CREATION IS SUPPLEMENTED THROUGH NATURE OR PROVIDENCE.

> *Nevertheless He did not leave Himself without witness, in that He did good, gave us rain from heaven and fruitful seasons, filling our hearts with food and gladness." (Acts 14:17)*[30]

Creation itself is a demonstration of the existence of God. Men make idols of the creation, rather than worship the Creator. General revelation is

---

[30] Creator and Sustainer of the world—harvests, rain, sun. Most religions have rituals to acknowledge some higher being.

sufficient to hold all men accountable to worship God, but not efficient to bring about the faith that saves. Men try to explain the creation without a Creator because they know that if there is a Creator, then there is someone who is higher than themselves, and they may be accountable to Him! So they explain the universe and our existence without God!

> *Only fools say in their hearts, "There is no God." They are corrupt, and their actions are evil; not one of them does good! (Psa. 14:1, NLT)*

## 4) THEY HAVE HUMAN CONSCIENCE.

The heathen have neither the light of the Law nor the light of the Gospel. They have the light of conscience (Rom. 1:19 [in their conscience]; 2:14,15).

General revelation is sufficient to hold all men accountable to worship God but not efficient to bring about the faith that saves. The conscience is the voice of God.

> *He will punish sin wherever it is found. He will punish the heathen when they sin, even though they never had God's written laws, for down in their hearts they know right from wrong. God's laws are written within them; their own conscience accuses them, or sometimes excuses them. (Rom. 2:12, NLT)*

> *They demonstrate that God's law is written in their hearts, for their own conscience and thoughts either accuse them or tell them they are doing right. (Rom 2:15, TLB)*

Even those who are not Christians from other religions and societies, have a right and wrong. Where did they get this from? From the conscience given to them by God Himself.

Rebellion against God corrupts. See Romans 1:18-32. Verse 18—**"*children of wrath*"**). Verses 19-21—men **knew** God. They suppress the truth of creation (vv. 18,21,32), exchange the truth for a lie (v. 25), worship the god of nature (v. 25; Psa. 19). General revelation of God's existence is not sufficient for true seekers, but rather the opposite.

People get worse and worse: Rom. 1:24, 26-28 (God **gave them up**); Rom. 1:18 (to reject God is to receive God's wrath, John 3:36); Romans 1:18-32; 2:8; 3:23; Ephesians 2:1-3; 4:18; 6:12; II Thessalonians 1:8-10.

## JESUS AND ETERNAL LIFE

The Scripture makes it very clear that one can only have eternal life through Jesus Christ: John 3:8,16,36; 5:24; 6:47-54; 14:6; I John 2:2,23; 3:8,23; 5:11,12; 4:14; 1:7; 25:46 (eternal life and eternal punishment); I <u>Tim. 2:5</u> (one Mediator).

> *But as many as received Him, to them He gave the right to become children of God, to those who believe in His name. (John 1:12)*

> *Jesus answered and said to him, "Most assuredly, I say to you, unless one is born again, he cannot see the kingdom of God." (John 3:3)*

> *And this is what God has testified: He has given us eternal life, and this Life is in his Son. Whoever has the Son has life; whoever does not have God's Son does not have life. (I John 5:11,12, NLT)*

> *... no other Name by which we must be saved. (Acts 4:12)*

## CONSEQUENCES OF REJECTION

What are the consequences of rejection of the revelation given to man?[31]

Jesus gives us an explanation of the judgment of the nations and of the righteous and the unrighteous.

> *Then He will also say to those on the left hand, "Depart from Me, you cursed, into the everlasting fire prepared for the devil and his angels." (Matt. 25:41)*

> *Professing to be wise, they became fools, and changed the glory of the incorruptible God into an image made like corruptible man —and birds and four-footed animals and creeping things. Therefore God also gave them up to uncleanness, in the lusts of their hearts, to dishonor their bodies among themselves, who exchanged the truth of God for the lie, and worshiped and served the creature rather than the Creator, who is blessed forever. Amen. For this reason God gave them up to vile passions. For even their women exchanged the natural use for what is against nature. Likewise also the men, leaving the natural use of the woman, burned in their lust for one another, men with men*

---

[31] John 3:16,36; Rom. 5:9;; I Thess. 1:10; II Thessalonians 1:8-10; John 3:18; 8:24; 11:25; Matthew 13:42,50; 25:41,45,46; Rev. 21:8; 14:11; 20:10

*committing what is shameful, and receiving in themselves the penalty of their error which was due. And even as they did not like to retain God in their knowledge, God gave them over to a debased mind, to do those things which are not fitting; being filled with all unrighteousness, sexual immorality, wickedness, covetousness, maliciousness; full of envy, murder, strife, deceit, evil-mindedness; they are whisperers, backbiters, haters of God, violent, proud, boasters, inventors of evil things, disobedient to parents, undiscerning, untrustworthy, unloving, unforgiving, unmerciful; who, knowing the righteous judgment of God, that those who practice such things are deserving of death, not only do the same but also approve of those who practice them. (Rom. 1:22-32)*

*He who overcomes will inherit these things, and I will be his God and he will be My son. But for the cowardly and unbelieving and abominable and murderers and immoral persons and sorcerers and idolaters and all liars, their part will be in the lake that burns with fire and brimstone, which is the second death. (Rev. 21:7-8, NASB)*

Heaven is a real place. So is hell! Matthew 25:46 (KJV): ***And these shall go away into everlasting punishment: but the righteous into life eternal.*** In Revelation 20:15, it is called a ***lake of fire, fire and brimstone*** (but rather fear Him Who is able to destroy both soul and body in hell, Matt. 10:28). It is called **outer darkness** (Matt. 8:12), **torment** (Rev. 14:10,11), ***wrath of God*** (Rom. 2:5; John 3:36), ***eternal destruction from the presence of the Lord*** (II Thess. 1:8-10). They are excluded from the Kingdom of God forever (***the unrighteous shall not inherit the Kingdom of God....*** READ I Corinthians 6:9,10—***they that do such things [works of the flesh as a lifestyle] shall not inherit the Kingdom of God*** (Gal. 5:19,20; see Luke 16:19-31, the rich man in hell).

## **HELL**

- "Gehenna" is used 12 times in the New Testament, 11 times by Christ Himself
- Everlasting punishment – Matt. 25:41,45; 13:42,50
- Lake of fire – Rev. 20:15
- Fire and brimstone – Matt. 3:12
- Destroys body and soul – Matt. 10:28
- Outer darkness – Matt. 8:12
- Torment – Rev. 14:10,11

- Wrath of God – Rom. 2:5; John 3:36
- Second death – Rev. 21:1-22; 20:11-14 (Rev. 20:7-15, no extinction, or else could be no second death)
- No probation after death
- Excluded from the Kingdom of God – I Cor. 6:9,10; Gal. 5:19,20
- Eternal: not age-long
- John 3:36 ("He that believeth on the Son has everlasting life; he that does not believe in the Son shall not see life; but the wrath of God abides on him" 8:24); 11:25 ("I am the Resurrection and the Life"); Matt. 13:42,50 (final harvest: angels to cast the tares "into a furnace of fire: there will be wailing and gnashing of teeth.")

## **THE LAST JUDGMENT**[32]

One more great universe-embracing event must take place before there can be eternal peace and righteousness, namely, the judgment of the impenitent dead. This is set forth in the last paragraph of this epoch-crowded chapter. A day of judgment, sometimes called "The Last Day," is referred to more often by our Lord than by all of the apostles and their writings put together (see Matt. 10:15; 11:22,24; 12:36; John 5:28,29; 6:39-54; 11:24; Heb. 9:27; 10:27). Christ is everywhere identified as the Judge (see especially Acts 17:31; John 5:22-27; II Tim. 4:1). Bishop Gore spoke for all the Church when he said, "It seems to me any believer in the God of the prophets, and of our Lord, must believe with them in a Day of God, as bringing the present age of human history to its climax" (*Belief in Christ*, p. 149; taken from *The Wycliffe Bible Commentary*, Electronic Database, copyright © 1962 by Moody Press).

## **UNIQUENESS OF CHRIST**

There is **no** Christ-less salvation!

**Example**: Cornelius, who was a Gentile and who was commended by God, yet needed salvation (Acts 11:14). It is God's heart that none should perish. Again, John 3:16 makes it clear: *God SO loved the world that those who believe in Him should not perish*. Second Peter 3:9 says, *"The Lord is ... not willing that any should perish, but that all should come to repentance."* That is why we preach the Gospel to glorify God and see sinners escape the pangs of hell (Acts 4:12).

---

[32] Rev. 20:11-14

> *He who believes in the Son has everlasting life; and he who does not believe the Son shall not see life, but the wrath of God abides on him. (John 3:36)*

Jesus said that He was going to prepare a place for us, that He would come again for those who are still living at His return to take us to be with Him.

> *Father, I desire that they also whom You gave Me may be with Me where I am, that they may behold My glory which You have given Me; for You loved Me before the foundation of the world. (John 17:24)*

The question needs to be asked: What happens to those who do not hear the Gospel? Will they be judged? They will be judged not because they refused the Gospel, but because they failed to live up to the light they had. God does not consign them to hell. That is where they have chosen to be.

> *... not willing that any should perish, but that all should come to repentance. (II Pet. 3:9)*

## APPLICATION

If we are to have the heart of Christ, we are to weep for the lost. We need to be moved with compassion as Christ. People are going to hell (some say at least 140,000 daily—69 men, women, teens per minute, 4,000 per hour) and we have the message to bring them redemption. Jesus has commanded the Church:

> *Go into all the world and preach the gospel to every creature ... signs shall follow, there will be tongues, and you shall cast out demons. (Mark 16:15)*

We need to go to the younger generation, the university students, political leaders, military, schools, neighbors, orthodox churches. We need to share the Gospel with them. Piety, sincerity, goodness are not enough (Acts 4:12; Rom. 10:13).

---

J. Hudson Taylor, who spent 50 years in China, said that in all that time he never met anyone who claimed to have lived up to the light he had.

## QUESTION ONE

<u>Is there a second chance?</u> Nothing in the teaching of Christ suggests the possibility (Luke 16:19-31), but the very opposite (Heb. 9:27).

## QUESTION TWO

<u>What if they do not hear the Gospel?</u> They will be judged not because they refused to believe the Gospel, but because they failed to live up to the light they had. God does not consign them to hell. That is where they belong. Romans 10:9-15: ... *that if you shall confess with your mouth the Lord Jesus....* Everyone *who believes in Him receives forgiveness of sins through His name.* Everyone who calls on the name of the Lord will be saved, not Buddha, Vishnu, or Krishna, or any other name (Rom. 10:13)!

- Not a "higher power"
- Fulfillment of Old Testament prophecy – Acts 2:16,25,34,39; 3:18,19,21,24
- For all mankind – I John 2:2; 4:14, "... the Father sent His Son to be the Savior or the world."

If Christ sent His Son to the world to die on the Cross, there is not another way. If there is salvation without Christ, there is no need of the Cross. What a price!

- God is just! He makes no mistakes. It would be just for God to send all of us to hell because of our sins. We all deserve it!
- Grace!! – Eph. 1:7; 2:5,7,8
- Resurrection: proof of the uniqueness of Christ and that God accepted the sacrifice of His Son for our sins, not only His sinless life
- Acts 17:31 – "God has given proof of this to all men by raising Christ from the dead."

## QUESTION THREE

<u>If we say there is another way, what is it?</u> Works? Religion? How can I get to heaven? There are only two religions: Cain (works) and Abel (faith and sacrifice).

- Only by special revelation, special acts of God and the preaching of the Gospel – Rom. 10:9-21 – Incarnation/Cross
- He will deal justly with those who have heard and those who have not heard.

## CONSEQUENCES OF REJECTION

- Luke 16:23 – rich man in hell
- Mark 3:29 – One who blasphemes the Holy Spirit has never forgiveness and is subject to eternal condemnation and is guilty of eternal sin (NIV)
- "Eternal destruction from the presence of the Lord" – II Thess. 1:9
- John 14:10b – "The words that I say to you are not just my own. Rather, it is the Father, living in Me, who is doing His work." When Jesus speaks, God speaks!
- Uniqueness of Christ: the divine record of His good works is also the record of His absolute Lordship!
- "If a man preach any other Gospel, let him be accursed" – Gal. 1:9,10,13
- He died, He rose again, He is the resurrection and the life – John 11:25 (I am the Resurrection and the Life)

## HEAVEN IS A PLACE, NOT A STATE ONLY

- John 14:6 (preparation – "abiding places"); Phil. 2:9-11; Eph. 1:20-23
- John 17:24 – "Father, I will that they also, whom you have given me, be with me where I am; that they may behold my glory which you have given me."
- Sermon on the Mount – Matt. 5:3,9-12

# Addendum III

# Six Reasons for Suffering[33]

1. **<u>Deepens and purifies our faith</u>** – II Cor. 1:8, 9 – makes heaven more desired (Rom. 5:3,4). We are to be a partaker of His holiness (Heb. 2:10; 5:8).

2. **<u>Increases our experience of God's glory</u>** (II Cor. 4:17,18; Rom. 8:18; Matt. 5:11,12)

3. **<u>*Suffering is the price of making others bold*</u>** (Phil. 1:14)

   *Continue earnestly in prayer, being vigilant in it with thanksgiving; 3 meanwhile praying also for us, that God would open to us a door for the word, to speak the mystery of Christ, for which I am also in chains, 4 that I may make it manifest, as I ought to speak. (Col. 4:2-4)*

4. **Suffering fills up what is lacking in Christ's afflictions** – Col. 1:24; Phil. 3:10 (counted worthy); Acts 5:41; Eph. 3:1-3 (Paul a prisoner of Rome)

   *Filling up what was left behind with Christ – Church suffering now… suffering for Christ. Paul… I am glad for I am participating in the sufferings of Christ that continue for His Body, the Church.*

   *I am glad when I suffer for you in my body, for I am participating in the sufferings of Christ that continue for his body, the church. (Col. 1:24, NLT)*

5. **Suffering initiates the mission command to go** – Acts 8:1; 1:8; 11:19
   - Studies show that the richer we are the smaller percentage of our income we give to church and missions. Poorest – 2.4%; Richest – 1.6%
   - Being arrested is an opportunity for the proclamation of the Gospel (Luke 12:12,13; Mark 13:9)

---

[33] Notes on pages 87-100 of *Let the Nations be Glad* by John Piper.

6. **The supremacy of Christ is shown (manifest) in suffering**
   - Paul's thorn – not removed – my grace is sufficient – II Cor. 12:9,10
   - Paul's power was the power of Christ – II Cor. 1:9 – not to rely on self but the power of God
   - Loss and suffering – joyfully accepted, shows the supremacy of God's worth – rejoice for your reward is great in heaven – Matt. 5:11,12
   - Reason for rejoicing: the worth of our reward in heaven is so much greater than all the suffering on earth.
   - II Cor. 12:9,10 – gladly boast
   - Rom. 5:2-4 – rejoice in suffering
   - Acts 5:41 – Apostles rejoice in suffering
   - Heb. 10:34 – plundering of property
   - I Pet. 4:13 – count it all joy
   - Psa. 3:3 – You are my glory and the lifter of my head.
   - Peter: we have left all! Matt. 19:17,29
   - This is the ultimate sacrifice in following Jesus. You will be repaid in the resurrection of the just (Luke 14:14). Your reward will be great (Matt. 5:12). Nothing can compare with the joy of walking in the Light with Jesus as opposed to walking in darkness without Him.
   - John 8:12 – To follow Jesus does include suffering – death, but the path is full of light and truth … with you to the end of the age (Matt. 28:20)
   - Even joy in the midst of sorrow and pain – John 15:12

# Addendum IV

# Prayer and World Missions: Paul's Prayer Requests

## INTRODUCTION

Biblical prayers are an energizing and powerful force in the universe. Scriptures and experience are full of many testimonies of prayer's influence on God, nations, men, and demons. In this addendum, we examine prayer and world missions. The questions to be answered are some of the specific Biblical requests given to us concerning effecting praying for missions today (Isa. 64:1-7; James 5:16-18 – imperfect channels – Elijah, Abraham, Moses, prophets, apostles); Zech. 10:1; I Tim. 2:3; Acts 6:4)

## PRAYER: NOT A MINISTRY OF THE CHURCH BUT THE MINISTRY OF THE CHURCH

First prayer that Jesus taught His disciples: *"Thy Kingdom Come..." – Missions prayer!* When Jesus wanted to build His Church, He began with a prayer meeting—Acts 1:14

- 10-day prayer meeting, preaching, 3,000 souls
- Following conversions – Acts 2:42,47
- Division in Church concerning care for widows – Acts 6:2-4
- When pollution drove out prayer in the temple, Jesus drove out pollution to bring back prayer into His House – Mark 11:11-18; Matt. 21;12-16

God's promises that His Word should not return void:

- Commandments: not grievous – "come unto Me ..."
- His promises are true and eternal

- I Sam. 12:23
- Luke 18:1
- Isaiah 64:1-7; James 5:16-18
- Acts 6:4 (leadership)
- I Tim. 2:3

Imperfect Vessels: Abraham (interceded for Sodom), Moses (people of Israel), Elijah, prophets, apostles

Where does it all begin? **At the Throne Room!** Even heathen who pray have had the inherent desire placed there by God.

## A. ETERNITY – BEFORE TIME[34]

Before time – Jesus in prayer. All prayer begins at the Throne Room – even heathen who pray have had the inherent desire placed there by God. Church Growth? Eph. 1:4; Rom. 8:29, 30

## B. DURING LIFETIME ON EARTH[35]

- John 17:18-20
- Isa. 53:12; cf. Luke 23:34 – "Father, forgive them …"
- Luke 23:42,43 – "Lord, remember me …"
- Acts 2:4-6 – Prayer – Power – Proclamation
- Jesus in Prayer: Luke 6:12; Matt. 4:23

## C. ETERNITY – PRESENT MINISTRY

- Intercessor: Jesus in Prayer[36]
- Early Church[37]

## SPECIFIC PRAYER REQUESTS OF JESUS

1. Thy Kingdom Come – Matt. 6:10
2. Laborers - Matt. 9:38; Luke 10:2; 6:12,13; Acts 13:2 (New Testament Church)

---

[34] Psa. 2:8; 22:27; 72:8; John 17:4,5
[35] Luke 6:12; 22:31-34,39-46; Heb. 5:7, 8
[36] Heb. 7:16,25 ("ever lives"); I John 2:1,2; Rom. 8:34,36; I Tim. 2:5; John 17:20
[37] Acts 1:14; 2:1-4; 3:3; 4:23-31; 6:3,4

When God has a man or woman who is willing to labor for Him, He will accomplish His purpose in that person and in relationship to the Kingdom of God—spiritually, not educationally. God does not begin with program but with man. The word **send them forth** in the original is **to kick them out" (ex baleo;** Matt. 9:38). It is sending laborers to the unreached people groups that they may hear that from around the throne there will be people from every tribe, nation, tongue, and people group (Rev. 5:9; John 17:20). And it begins on our knees, not in our head **The Holy Spirit said ...** (Acts 13:2).

In considering prayer and world missions, we want to look at some of the prayer requests of Paul the apostle, the writer of two-thirds of the NT New Testament. He is an example of a man totally dependent upon God in the power of the Holy Spirit for His life and ministry. He knew that prayer was foundational to his ministry, as it was in the life of Christ.

> *Yet I dare not boast about anything except what Christ has done through me. (Rom. 15:18)*

> *For I am the least of the apostles, that am not meet to be called an apostle, because I persecuted the church of God. For I have worked harder than any of the other apostles; yet it was not I but God who was working through me by his grace. (I Cor. 15:9,10)*

## SPECIFIC PRAYER REQUESTS

### 1) THE FREEDOM OF SPEECH & BOLDNESS OF UTTERANCE

Paul was asking for prayer that he would be filled with holy boldness and courage in proclaiming the Gospel—that he would do it without fear or doubt. The context of this request is that of spiritual warfare, satanic opposition! There will always be opposition when the Gospel is preached.

> *... praying always with all prayer and supplication in the Spirit, being watchful to this end with all perseverance and supplication for all the saints—and for me, that utterance may be given to me, that I may open my mouth boldly to make known the mystery of the gospel ... (Eph. 6:18,19)*

> *But if our gospel be hid, it is hid to them that are lost: Satan, who is the god of this world, has blinded the minds of those who don't believe. They are unable to see the glorious light of the Good News. (II Cor. 4:3,4)*

The other apostles also experienced (Acts 2:4; 4:13,29,31) what he had experienced (14:3; 28:31). Here are some results of the Word of God being proclaimed with boldness:

> *And when they had prayed, the place where they were assembled together was shaken; and they were all filled with the Holy Spirit, and they spoke the word of God with boldness. (Acts 4:31)*

> *The word of God kept on spreading; and the number of the disciples continued to increase greatly in Jerusalem, and a great many of the priests were becoming obedient to the faith. (Acts 6:7)*

> *But the word of the Lord continued to grow and to be multiplied. (Acts 12:24)*

## 2) THE WORD TO BE GLORIFIED

> *Finally, brethren, pray for us, that the Word of the Lord may run swiftly and be glorified, just as it is with you ... to be honored wherever it goes (NLT) ... be extolled and triumph (AMP). (II Thess. 3:1)*

> *When the Gentiles heard this, they began rejoicing and glorifying the word of the Lord; and as many as had been appointed to eternal life believed. And the word of the Lord was being spread through the whole region. (Acts 13:48, NASB)*

Paul asked for prayer that the Word of God would have *free course* ... and go forward *without hindrances.* Paul is asking for prayer that his preaching would be Word-centered, not preacher-centered, and that the Word would be magnified in those that would hear. Some of the results when the Word was preached, even before Paul was converted, are evident. **The Word of God increased**(Acts 6:7,12-24; 13:48,49). When the **Name of Jesus** was proclaimed there were life-changing results (Acts 4:2,4,7,17,20,31; 5:9,20,28,42; 6:2,7; 8:4; 9:27).

## 3) FREEDOM FROM DANGER – PROTECTION AND DELIVERANCE

> *Now I beg you, brethren, through the Lord Jesus Christ, and through the love of the Spirit, that you strive together with me in prayers to God for me, that I may be delivered from those in Judea who do not believe. (Rom. 15:30,31)*

Prayer was instrumental in Peter's deliverance from prison (Acts 12:1-6).

> *Peter was therefore kept in prison, but constant prayer was offered to God for him by the church. (Acts 12:5)*

> *Now Peter continued knocking; and when they opened the door and saw him, they were astonished. ... he declared to them how the Lord had brought him out of the prison. (Acts 12:16,17)*

Paul was so thankful to the Philippians for praying for him. And yet he said that all the things that happened to him were **for the furtherance of the Gospel** (Phil. 1:2,13).

> *For I know that as you pray for me and the Spirit of Jesus Christ helps me, this will lead to my deliverance. (Phil. 1:19)*

## 4) FREEDOM TO SERVE: MINISTRY TO BE ACCEPTED AND ACCEPTABLE

> *Now I beg you, brethren, through the Lord Jesus Christ, and through the love of the Spirit, that you strive together with me in prayers to God for me ... that my service for Jerusalem may be acceptable to the saints. (Rom. 15:30,31)*

## 5) OPEN DOORS

> *Continue earnestly in prayer, being vigilant in it with thanksgiving; meanwhile praying also for us, that God would open to us a door for the word, to speak the mystery of Christ, for which I am also in chains, that I may make it manifest, as I ought to speak. (Col. 4:2-4)*

Paul experienced the results of those prayers!

> *There is a wide open door for a great work here, although many oppose me. (I Cor. 16:9)*
> *The Lord opened a door of opportunity for me. (II Cor. 2:12)*
> *I am hoping to come unto you through your prayers. (Philemon 22)*

It is God that opens and it is God that closes doors.

> *Furthermore, when I came to Troas to preach Christ's gospel, and a door was opened to me by the Lord ... (II Cor. 2:12)*

> *Now when they had gone through Phrygia and the region of Galatia, they were forbidden by the Holy Spirit to preach the word in Asia. After they had come to Mysia, they tried to go into Bithynia, but the Spirit did not permit them. (Acts 16:6,7)*

> *And to the angel of the church in Philadelphia write, "These things says He who is holy, He who is true, He who has the key of David, He who opens and no one shuts, and shuts and no one opens. I know your works. See, I have set before you an open door, and no one can shut it." (Rev. 3:7,8)*

### Illustration of Prayer and Missions

While Peter was praying in Joppa, the Lord gave him a vision. Cornelius was praying in Caesarea and was told by the Holy Spirit to seek for Peter (Acts 10:4,5). Peter responded to the call of the Spirit to preach to Cornelius and his household. They were converted, and were baptized with the Holy Spirit. Thus, the door to the Gentiles was opened (Acts 10). One can see prayer as being critical in the salvation of the lost!

**Question**: What area is God calling you to pray about? What city? What country? What group of people? Begin in intercession and in prayer! We have seen God do some miraculous interventions in specific answers to prayer for specific cities and countries.

## 6) THANKSGIVING TO GOD

Paul asks for prayer, for when it is answered, there will be more praise given to God, more people responding in worship—all for the glory of God! This is what God ultimately seeks: worshipers (John 4:21-23).

> *... you also helping together in prayer for us, that thanks may be given by many persons on our behalf for the gift granted to us through many. (II Cor. 1:11)*

> *For all things are for your sakes, that grace, having spread through the many, may cause thanksgiving to abound to the glory of God. (II Cor. 4:15)*

## 7) CLEAR CONSCIENCE

Here the apostle Paul asks for prayer that he may live a godly life! He recognized that he was not above temptation, that having a leadership position in the Church would not exempt him from being tempted of evil. It is a lesson for us all! If Jesus was tempted in ***all points like as we are, yet without sin***, how much more do we need to live a holy life, obedient to the Word, and fully dependent upon the Holy Spirit to live a victorious life!

> *Keep praying for us that we might live a noble life, acting honorably and honestly in all things with a clear and clean conscience. (Heb. 13:18)*

> *Brothers, I have lived before God in all good conscience up to this day ... (Acts 23:1)*

> *So I always take pains to have a clear conscience toward God and man ... (Acts 24:16)*

> *For our boast is this: the testimony of our conscience that we behaved in the world with simplicity, and godly sincerity, not by earthly wisdom but by the grace of God and supremely toward you. (II Cor. 1:12)*

Though he was not perfect, he admonished us to follow him as he followed Christ.

> *Follow my example, as I follow the example of Christ. (II Cor. 11:1)*

> *Keep putting into practice all you learned and received from me— everything you heard from me and saw me doing. Then the God of peace will be with you. (Phil. 4:9)*

> *Brethren, pray for us [his concluding statement]! (I Thess. 5:25)*

There are many Old Testament illustrations of how prayer and intercession were instrumental in changing the course of history. It was God, through the intercession of Esther, who moved the hand of Ahasuerus who spared the Jews from annihilation (Esther 8). God moved upon Pharaoh through the intercession of Moses and set the Jews free after 40 years of bondage! King Darius, upon the return of the Jews to Judea gave permission for Jerusalem to be rebuilt *...that they may offer sacrifices ... **AND PRAY FOR THE LIFE OF THE KING, AND HIS SONS*** (Ezra 6:10). Artaxerxes granted the request of Ezra for some of the Jews to return to Jerusalem, ***because the gracious hand of the Lord was upon him*** (Ezra 7:6). Because of the intercessory petition to Artaxerxes by Nehemiah he was granted permission to return to Jerusalem to rebuild the city, ***and the king granted them to me*** *according to the good hand of my God upon me* (Neh. 2:8). Again, notice that God answered the prayers of His servants because His hand was upon them.

## CONCLUSION

We are called to not only pray, *"**Bless the missionaries,**"* but to offer specific prayer requests that are appropriate and necessary for the work of the ministry. Some people are out in the battlefield, while others are supporting those in the frontline of ministry. All are important to the mission. The hidden members of the body are necessary for the outward members to function, e.g., heart, pituitary and thyroid glands, lungs, etc. Without them functioning in unison, we would not have a healthy body! Every member in the Body of Christ will be rewarded not for how many pounds the servant received nor for the results of the sowing, but for being a ***good and faithful servant*** with the pounds given (Matt. 25:21). David assessed those who supported the soldiers in the frontline ministry of equal value. They shared the rewards of the victory.

We cannot be a Billy Graham touching millions of lives, but the dividing of spoils of the reward of the great harvest will be shared with those who are unseen (hidden parts of the Body) in making his ministry a reality—those who intercede in prayer, clerks, donors, secretaries, technicians, media personnel, bookkeepers, etc. ***One sows, one waters, but God gives the increase*** (I Cor. 3:6,7). What an encouragement for us! (I Cor. 12:12-14)

> *For who will heed you in this matter? But as his part is who goes down to the battle, so shall his part be who stays by the supplies ["stayed by the stuff," KJV] they shall share alike. (I Sam. 30:24)*

## EXAMPLES OF INTERCESSORS

- Abraham – Gen. 18:23-32; cf. Jer. 5:1
- Moses – Exodus 32:30-35
- Anna – Luke 2:36,37
- Epaphras – Col. 4:12

### A. <u>God's Priority</u>[38]

---

[38] Heb. 7:25; Rom. 8:26,27; Acts 2:42; Luke 18:1; Jude 20; Isa. 62:1-7

## B. God's Search – God's Marvels[39]

- Judgment – Psa. 106:23 (with Moses) – Gen. 18:23-32 (Abraham); cf. Jer. 5:1; Luke 2:36,37 (Anna); Col. 4:2 (Epaphras)
- Faith: Matt. 8:10 – *I have not found so great faith, no not in Israel* (centurion)
- Unbelief – Mark 6:6 – *He could do no mighty miracles because of their unbelief*
- Challenge
- Psa. 109:4 – *For my love, they are my adversaries … but I give myself unto prayer …*
- Psa. 126:5,6 – *They that sow in tears shall reap in joy … He that goeth forth and weepeth, bearing precious seed shall countless come again with rejoicing bringing His sheaves with him.*
- Some "*stay by the stuff*" (I Sam. 30:24). You shall receive an reward for the battle equal with the frontline warriors!

**Final**: Rev. 5:9; 7:10; 19:1-9 – Worship, the end of Missions!

---

[39] Isa. 50:2; 59:16; 64:7; Ezek. 22:30

# Addendum V

# One Another

We are the Body of Christ (Eph. 4:3).

- **_Admonish one another_** ("teach and counsel each other," LB) – Col. 3:16; Rom. 15:14
- **_Bear with one another in love_** ("making allowances for each other's faults because of your love for Christ," NLB) – Eph. 4:2
- **_Comfort (care for) one another_** ("encourage," NLT) – I Thess. 4:18
- **_Confess your faults one to another_** – James 5:16
- **_Consider one another better than ourselves_** ("count others more significant than yourselves," AMP; "motivate, stimulate, show honor," LB; "thinking of others better than yourself," NLB; "practice playing second fiddle," MSG) – Phil. 2:3; cf. Rom. 12:10

*Don't be selfish; don't try to impress others. Be humble, thinking of others as better than yourselves. Don't look out only for your own interests, but take an interest in others, too. You must have the same attitude that Christ Jesus had. (Phil. 2:3-5, NLB)*

- **_Edify (strengthen, encourage) one another_** – *I Thess. 5:11*
- **_Exhort one another_** ("warning, urging," AMP) – Heb. 10:25
- **_Forbear one another_** ("show meekness, making allowances with faults because you love one another; ready to pardon," MSG) – Eph. 4:2
- **_Forgive one another_** – Eph. 4:3; Col. 3:13; Matt. 6:14,15; Mark 11:24,25; Heb. 10:24; 10:25; I Thess. 5:11
- **_Live in harmony with one another_** (adjust yourself to people; give yourselves to humble tasks) – Rom. 12:16
- **_Love (be kindly affectionate toward) one another_** ("don't run up debts, except for the huge debt of love to one another," MSG) – Rom. 13:8; I John 3:11,23; 4:11,12; I Thess. 4:9; I Pet. 1:22; II John 5
- **_Pray for one another_**

*Confess your sins to each other and pray for each other so that you may be healed. The earnest prayer of a righteous person has great power and produces wonderful results. (James 5:16, NLT)*

- **<u>Prefer (in honor) one another</u>** ("be good friends who love deeply; practice playing second fiddle," MSG)

    *Love each other with genuine affection, and take delight in honoring each other. (Rom. 12:10, NLT)*

    *Therefore, accept each other just as Christ has accepted you so that God will be given glory. (Rom. 15:7, NLT)*

    *For you have been called to live in freedom, my brothers and sisters. But don't use your freedom to satisfy your sinful nature. Instead, use your freedom to serve one another in love. (Gal. 5:13)*

- **<u>Seek to do good to one another and to everyone</u>**

    *… and to esteem them very highly in love for their work's sake. Be at peace among yourselves. … See that no one pays back evil for evil, but always try to do good to each other and to all people. (I Thess. 5:13,15)*

- **<u>Speak kindly (be pleasant) to one another</u>**

    *Let your conversation be gracious and attractive so that you will have the right response for everyone. (Col. 4:6)*

- **<u>Teach and admonish one another</u>**

    *… train one another with all insight, intelligence, wisdom and spiritual things. And whatever you do or say, do it as a representative of the Lord Jesus, giving thanks through him to God the Father. (Col. 3:16,17)*

- **<u>Warn one another</u>**

    *You must warn each other every day, while it is still "today," so that none of you will be deceived by sin and hardened against God. (Heb. 3:13,14, NLT)*

- **<u>Motivate one another</u>**

    *Let us think of ways to motivate one another to acts of love and good works. (Heb. 10:24 – NLT)*

Are you a foot washer? Will you deny yourself, cover the faults of others, and show meekness without recognition or even thanks?

> *But the Holy Spirit produces this kind of fruit in our lives: love, joy, peace, patience, kindness, goodness, faithfulness, gentleness, and self-control. There is no law against these things! (Gal. 5:22,23, NLT)*

> *Always be humble and gentle. Be patient with each other, making allowance for each other's faults because of your love. (Eph. 4:2, NLT)*

**Can we do it?** Yes, only by the grace of God and the Spirit of God!

*I know how to be abased and live humbly in straitened circumstances, and I know also how to enjoy plenty and live in abundance. I have learned in any and all circumstances the secret of facing every situation, whether well-fed or going hungry, having a sufficiency and enough to spare or going without and being in want. I have strength for all things in Christ who empowers me [I am ready for anything and equal to anything through Him who infuses inner strength unto me; I am self-sufficient in Christ's sufficiency]. (Phil. 4:12, AMP)*

CPSIA information can be obtained
at www.ICGtesting.com
Printed in the USA
FSOW02n1518190815
10067FS